# GAMES, GOALS
# & PURPOSES

# KEYS TO THE KINGDOM SERIES
## POCKET EDITION

Published from
Mardukite Borsippa HQ, San Luis Valley, Colorado
Mardukite Academy & Systemology Society
*for spiritual or philosophical purposes only*

# GAMES, GOALS & PURPOSES

### Systemology
### Advanced Training Course
### Manual #2

As presented by Joshua Free
to the Systemology Society

THE JOSHUA FREE IMPRINT
JFI PUBLICATIONS

This manual is restricted to students on
*The Systemology Advanced Training Course*
that have already completed the
*"Pathway to Ascension" Professional Course*

References to prerequisite material:
*"The Secret of Universes" (AT #1)*
*"Eliminating Barriers" (PC-7)*
*"Conquest of Illusion" (PC-8)*
*"Games & Universes" (PC-12)*

Full use of this manual may also require:
*"Systemology Biofeedback"* and
*"Systemology Procedures"*

<u>*Advanced Manuals should be studied in the*</u>
<u>*sequential order in which they are numbered.*</u>

First Edition Pocket Paperback — *February 2024*

**mardukite.com**

# *The Keys to the Kingdom are Yours for the Taking!*

The official Mardukite Systemology "Advanced Training Course" is now available in print for the first time.

Those Seekers that have completed the "Pathway to Ascension" Systemology Professional Course can now access the upper-level teachings of our tradition.

This book is not for everyone... This is the second manual for Level-7.

Never before has Joshua Free presented this material outside the confines of the Mardukite NexGen Systemology Society.

Learn how to expertly apply our spiritual technology toward reaching higher levels of Awareness and Beingness than ever before thought possible for humanity on planet Earth.

Each of the "Keys to the Kingdom" Advanced Training Course Manuals will further a Seekers reach on the Pathway leading out of this Universe.

## The Pathway to Ascension
Professional Course Lesson Booklet Series

#1 – *Increasing Awareness (Level-0)*
#2 – *Thought & Emotion (Level-0)*
#3 – *Clear Communication (Level-0)*
#4 – *Handling Humanity (Level-1)*
#5 – *Free Your Spirit (Level-2)*
#6 – *Escaping Spirit-Traps (Level-2)*
#7 – *Eliminating Barriers (Level-3)*
#8 – *Conquest of Illusion (Level-3)*
#9 – *Confronting the Past (Level-4)*
#10 – *Lifting the Veils (Level-4)*
#11 – *Spiritual Implants (Level-5)*
#12 – *Games and Universes (Level-5)*
#13 – *Spiritual Energy (Level-6)*
#14 – *Spiritual Machinery (Level-6)*
#15 – *The Arcs of Infinity (Level-6)*
#16 – *Alpha Thought (Level-6)*

## Keys to the Kingdom
Advanced Training Course Manuals

#1 – *The Secret of Universes (Level-7)*
#2 – *Games, Goals & Purposes (Level-7)*
#3 – *The Jewel of Knowledge (Level-7)*
#4 – *Implanted Universes (Level-7)*

Advanced Training Supplemental Booklets

#1 – *Systemology Biofeedback*
#2 – *Systemology Procedures*

# TABLET OF CONTENTS

INTRODUCTION TO THE MANUAL

A.T. MANUAL #2:
GAMES, GOALS & PURPOSES

APPENDIX

"MANY YEARS AGO, I REALIZED
THAT 'THE WAY OUT' WOULD
SYSTEMATICALLY RESEMBLE
THE ROUTES BY WHICH WE
ORIGINALLY DESCENDED."
—*Joshua Free*
*Backtrack Lectures, 2023*

# INTRODUCTION TO
# THE MANUAL

This manual is restricted to students on
*The Systemology Advanced Training Course*
that have already completed the
*"Pathway to Ascension" Professional Course*

References to prerequisite material:
*"The Secret of Universes" (AT #1)*
*"Eliminating Barriers" (PC-7)*
*"Conquest of Illusion" (PC-8)*
*"Games & Universes" (PC-12)*

Full use of this manual may also require:
*"Systemology Biofeedback"* and
*"Systemology Procedures"*

# THE SYSTEMOLOGY
## ADVANCED TRAINING COURSE
### MANUAL SERIES

*Mardukite Systemology* is a new evolution in Human understanding about the "systems" governing *Life, Reality,* the *Universe* and all *Existences.* It is also a *Spiritual Path* used to transcend the Human experience and reach "*Ascension.*"

This is an *Advanced Training (AT)* course manual detailing *upper-levels* of our spiritual philosophy. It is intended to assist *advancing* a *Seeker's* personal progress toward the *upper-most levels* of the *Pathway.*

This manual follows after our *Professional Course* series of lessons—available as individual booklets, or collected in two volumes titled "*The Pathway to Ascension*" The *Professional Course* follows after material given in the *Basic Course* booklets, or "*Fundamentals of Systemology*" volume.

The systematic methodology that we use to assist an individual to increase their *"Actualized Awareness"* (and reach gradually higher toward their *"Spiritual Ascension"*) is referred to as *"The Pathway"* — and that individual is called a *"Seeker."*

To receive the greatest benefit from this manual: it is expected that a *Seeker* will already be familiar with the fundamental concepts and terminology (previously relayed in the *Basic Course* and *Professional Course* lessons) of our *applied philosophy.*

As a *Seeker* increases their *Awareness* in this lifetime, their spiritual *"Knowingness"* also increases—which is to say their *certainty* on *Life*, on this and other *Universes*, and on *realizing Self* as an unlimited "spiritual being" *having* an enforced restrictive "human experience." A *Seeker* also *knowingly* increases their command and control of the "human experience." And this is a part of what is meant by *"Actualized Awareness."*

## CHARTING FLIGHTS ON THE PATHWAY

Although there is a systematic structure to *fragmentation,* the personal journey experienced along the *Pathway* will be different for each *Seeker.* For example, certain areas will seem more *"turbulent"* or difficult for one *Seeker* than another. We tend to say that these areas have more *"charge"* on them—or that they are more *"heavily charged."* It is best to handle such areas when you are already feeling "good" and not in a situation (or condition) where that specific area is consistently being *"triggered"* or *"restimulated."*

As an applied philosophy, *Systemology* "theory" can be easily utilized in the "laboratory" of the "world-at-large" in everyday life. This is implied within the basic instruction of each lesson. Unlike other "sciences" that conduct experiments by making a change to some "objective variable" *out there* and waiting to see an effect, our focus is the individual (or *Observer*) themselves, and how *they* affect the "*Reality*" perceived.

Our philosophy is applied by using specific exercises and systematic techniques. These "*processes*" provide the most stable personal gain (and *realizations*) for each area; but only when actually applied with a *Seeker's* full "*presence*" and *Awareness*. Hundreds of such *processes* may be found in the "*Pathway to Ascension*" (*Professional Course*) material.

Applying a technique is called "*running a process.*" *Processes* are designed with very simple instructions or "*command-lines.*" To *run* a *processing command-line*, a *Seeker* may be assisted by the communication of that *line* from a "*Co-Pilot*" (as in "*Traditional Piloting*"). But even then, a *Seeker* must still personally "input" the *command* as *Self*. For this reason—and quite thankfully—*Solo-Processing* is possible.

## TAKING FLIGHT ON THE PATHWAY

*Processing Techniques* are intended to treat the *Spiritual Being* or *Alpha-Spirit*; the individual themselves. The *"command-lines"* are *directed to* the individual themselves—not some *mental machinery* of theirs, and not even a *Biofeedback* metering device.

*Systematic Processing* is applied by the *Alpha-Spirit*—who then *Self-directs* command of their "Mind-System" or "body" (*genetic-vehicle*), both of which are "constructs" that the *Alpha-Spirit* (*Self*, or the "I-AM" *Awareness unit*) operates, but neither of which is actually *Self*. *Fragmentation* causes *Humans* to falsely identify *Self* as the "*Mind*" or even a "*Body*."

Some *processes* can be treated quite lightly at first; others may require a bit of working at in order to get "*running*" well. It is important to set aside a period of time when you can be dedicated to your studies and *processing*. This period of time is referred to as a *"processing session."* When a *process* does start *running* well, it is important to be able to complete it to a satisfactory *"end-point."*

*Processing* allows us to be able to *actually* "look" at *things* and even determine the *considerations* we have made—or attitudes we have decided—about *Reality* as a result of those experiences.

It doesn't do us much good to simply "glance"—or to *restimulate* something uncomfortable and then quickly *withdraw* from it once again, leaving more of our *attention* yet again behind and held fixedly on it.

Generally speaking, a *Seeker* continues to *run* a *process* so long as something is "happening"—which is to say, the *process* is still producing a change. Usually this is evident by the type of "answers" that a *command-line* prompts a *Seeker* to originate from the database of their own *Mind-System*.

*Processing Command-Lines* ("PCL") are not "magic words"; they do not "do" anything on their own. They systematically assist a *Seeker* to direct their own attention toward increasing *Awareness.*

A *Seeker* may also cease to generate new "data" from a *process* without reaching an *"ultimate" realization* as an *"end-point."* It is possible that additional "layers" (or even other "areas") require handling before anything "deeper" is accessible. If this is the case, end the *process.* But, if a *Seeker* is *withdrawing* from something uncomfortable that was incited or stirred up, then a *process* is *run* until they feel "good" about it.

One of the benefits to *Flying-Solo* on the *Pathway* is that the *processing* is entirely *Self-determined.* This naturally provides a certain built-in "safety" for a practitioner. Anything you *restimulate* by *Self-determinism* is *your thing*. It is not triggered or incited by some external *"other-determined"* influences (or other "source-points") that make you an *effect*. It can be more easily handled in *processing*—or you can simply let things "cool down" and come back to it again in another *session*.

While it may seem "mysterious" to beginners, a *Seeker* gets a sense for knowing how long to *run* a *process* only with practice. Once you have spent some time actually applying material from *"The Pathway to Ascension"* Professional Course, there are many aspects of it that become "second nature" because they are, in fact, a part of our true original native nature. All we have done in *Systemology* is *"reverse engineer"* the routes of *creation* and *consideration* that are already *our own*.

*Advanced Manuals should be studied in the sequential order in which they are numbered.*

# SYSTEMOLOGY LEVEL-7

We are publishing *"upper-level"* *Systemology* in 2024 for the very first time. Its application is dependent on a *Seeker* reaching a stable point of *"Beta-Defragmentation."* This requires proper use of materials for previous *processing-levels*—as given in the *"Pathway to Ascension" Professional Course*. Of course, we don't refer to such an individual as *"defragmented"*—which only further reinforces that *something* exists to *defragment*—but instead, as having reached a *Beta-state* of *Self-Honesty*. This "state" *must* be reached in order to go further.

Up to this point, a *Seeker* has become *"better-abled"* in the *game* of *"Being Human."* They have learned to play the *game* of *Beta-Existence* better—while still *on Earth*, and possibly still quite fixated on a

"*Human Body.*" Yet, the completion of *Systemology Level-6* is still a stable point of accomplishment—and well above the level of *Awareness* maintained by the "standard-issue" *Human Condition.* The individual is less likely to fall into as many *traps* and is more able to "brush off" most additional *fragmentation* before it accumulates.

"*Alpha-Defragmentation*" is what the "*Keys to the Kingdom*" *Advanced Training Course* manuals pertain to. Our aim is still for "*metahuman destinations.*" The goal of *Systemology Level-7* is to "safely" deliver (or *Pilot*) a *Seeker* to the *next plateau* "in sight" from the stable point already reached. There is, of course, something of a *chasm* between these points. So, it is necessary for a *Seeker* to be certain they have relieved themselves of enough "baggage" and "weight" (of *spiritual fragmentation*) in order to get enough "lift" for their ascent.

In the past, a few have even stumbled upon this point of *"crossing the abyss"* within their own traditions. But without *defragmentation*, their new-found vigor and horsepower causes them to just more quickly and deeply get lost in various distracting spiritual detours and intellectual tangents; or even fall back to old patterns, if they cannot maintain *Self-Honesty*.

This *chasm* is *not* a pitfall for *processing* mistakes—or even an *actual* barrier. But it is a "drop-off" point that many *perceive* upon reaching this part of their journey. It is sometimes enough to keep a *Seeker* from going further on the *Pathway*, fearing that they risk their existing gains. Therefore, we held off presenting the *upper-levels* until our presentation/communication of the *Pathway* had been perfected—and *Seekers* could approach this material with greater *certainty* and *ability-to-confront* its *reality*.

An *advanced Seeker* is likely to spend many months, and over *100 processing-hours*, on *Systemology Level-7*.

The *four* manuals—*"The Secret of Universes," "Games, Goals & Purposes," "The Jewel of Knowledge"* and *"Implanted Universes"*—should be treated as a single "unit" of uninterrupted work. This doesn't mean handling it as a single *session*—nor are all *Seekers* in a position to take a *retreat* from their *lives*. But daily *restimulation,* or other distractions, can significantly affect progress at this stage. Completing *Level-7* may require longer and more frequent *sessions* to achieve the same steady gains that one is previously used to.

*Systemology Level-7* concerns primarily *"Games"*—which is also to say *"Universes."* On the *Standard Model, "Games and Universes"* is plotted at *"6.0"*—subordinate to the *"Alpha Thought"* (*"7.0"*) required to *postulate* or *create* the *"Game/*

*Universe*" into existence. This is senior to "*Intention*" at "5.0"—which is, of course, dependent upon some "*game-condition*" for any other *consideration* to occur. [This full description provides a perspective for just what "*upper-level*" part of the *Pathway* we are now treating with *Systemology Level-7*.]

_References to prerequisite materials_:
PC Lesson-7, "Eliminating Barriers"
PC Lesson-8, "Conquest of Illusion"
PC Lesson-12, "Games & Universes"
AT Manual #1, "The Secret of Universes"

# A.T. MANUAL #2
# GAMES, GOALS
# & PURPOSES

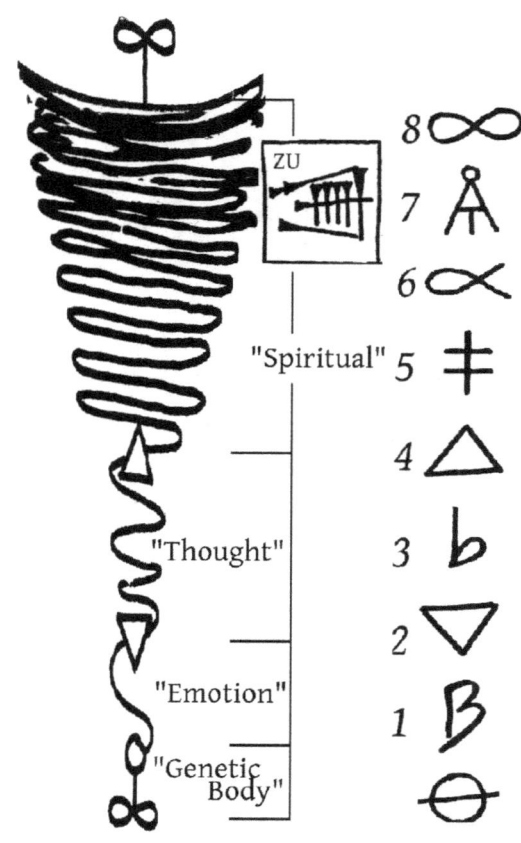

ZU

8  ∞

7

6

"Spiritual"  5

4

3

"Thought"

2

"Emotion"

"Genetic
Body"

## THE GAMES OF ALPHA-SPIRITS

After reading *"The Secret of Universes"* (*AT Manual #1*), a *Seeker* realizes the full scope of *"Games"* and *"Universes,"* and that it is beyond, or *"exterior"* to, what we classify as *"Beta-Awareness"* and *"Beta-Existence."* At *Systemology Level-7*, we are treating what *defines "Beta-Existence"* and our *perceived* "place" *within* it.

On the *Standard Model,* *"Games and Universes"* are plotted at *"6."* They are *below* the level of *"Alpha Thought"* (at *"7"*) that is required to *postulate/create* them into *existence.* *Games* are *above* the level of our *"Intention"* (at *"5"*)—which is also to say *"decision"* and *"choice,"* since such is generally dependent on *considerations* of a *game-condition.* To translate this as an *Alpha-Awareness* state: we could also refer to *"6"* as the *"Spirit of Play."*

The *creation* of *game-conditions* is the first point of true *fragmentation* for an *Alpha-Spirit*. This activity is directly inspired (or incited) by *The Jewel of Knowledge* (see *AT Manual #1 and #3*), which is our first real experience (and *Implant*) as a *Spiritual Being*. Though while in one's own "*Home Universe*," where one was *knowingly playing a game* with one's own *creations/illusions*, there didn't seem to be much *fragmentation*.

However, *The Jewel of Knowledge* lays in our first "*implanted*" *considerations*, which we naively used to formulate our first *postulate*: "there *must* be a *game*." As soon as we began to experience "*Shared Universes*" with others, the *game-conditions* became an intermediate between our *Alpha-Thought* and whatever we are *doing*. Therefore, the *Alpha-Spirit* has been "*playing a game*" for essentially the entirety of its *existence*.

We have realized (from *AT Manual #1*)

that shared *reality-agreements* about *game-conditions* are what *creates* a *Universe*. Within that *Universe*, there may be many *smaller-games* or *personality-phases* that one might *play*—but of which are all still subject to the grand *Game* that defines parameters or boundaries of that *Universe*; and by this we mean the *limitations* and *barriers* that are imposed on (and eventually *agreed to* by) an *Alpha-Spirit* in order to *have* some kind of *"playing piece"* for *communication* and *action* within that *Game-Universe*.

The main source of *Alpha-Fragmentation* occurs when the *Alpha-Spirit* *"collapses"* or *"merges"* all of their *considerations* for *Games and Universes* into a singular *Beta-Existence*. This occurs *knowingly* through *agreement*, and is encouraged *unknowingly* through *Implanting*; but at basic, the thing that is most *"wrong"* with us, is an inability (or unwillingness) to *separate Self* from the *Game* of *Beta-Existence*—to properly distinguish the differences between, for example, *this Physical Universe* and our *Personal Universe*. Because we have come to falsely accept that *this* is the "*only Game* in town" and that there is no where else "to go."

All *games* are based on *illusion*—hence all *games* are subject to, and propagate, *fragmentation*. For example, the *true* basic native state of an *Alpha-Spirit* is "*All-Knowing*" or pure "*Knowingness*." But this is not workable as a *game-condition*, so we must *lie* to ourselves, and maintain some degree of "*Not-Knowing*" in order to have a *game*. Thus, *game-conditions* are all *lies*; which is to say, *fragmentation* of our *true* native *Self-Honesty*.

While operating in one's own *Home Universe*, we *knowingly* decided to "*Not-Know*" for a certain period in order to manage all "sides" of an entire *Game* (*Universe*). *Fragmentation* occurs when we continuously and compulsively remain

"*Not-Knowing*" thereafter. In *Shared-Universes*, we even set up "*hidden parts*" of ourselves to keep running/operating *unknowingly* and *automatically*. This is how our total *Actualized Awareness* becomes reduced. We are still as potentially powerful as we always have been, but more of our *Awareness* has been *fragmented*—redirected or set on automatic—and is not *Self-Determined* (meaning, not under our control).

In the earliest days of our *systemological research*, what is now generally known as "*systematic processing*" first started as "*Games Processing.*" Although "*processing command-lines*" ("PCL") are often alternated to get the "*fragmented charge*" off of two opposing *considerations* (and/or alternated to better refocus and direct *attention*), the actual gains come from *processing-out "game-conditions"*; we aren't *defragmenting "truth."*

For example: the PCL "*what could you*

*know?"* has quite limited workability; yet an individual improves on *"what could you not-know?"* Trying to educate or *process* toward states of *truth* directly doesn't seem to work. It is either not accepted fully, or the information itself is not enough to override the *considerations* of *untruth* that result from *agreements* and/or *actions* against our basic native state.

The *apparent* "seriousness" of *Life* only enters into *consideration* when we "forget" that we are *playing a game*. This does not mean to say, *"It's all just a game; therefore, doesn't matter."* But, it *matters* to the degree that we consider our experience of the *Game of Life* as *real*.

Whether we consider *"games"* as something to *"do,"* or as a purely competitive activity, both tendencies seem to stem from *The Jewel of Knowledge* (at the "beginning" of our participation in *creation*). Even at upper-levels of *Beingness*, *"To Create"* is a *"doingness"* in order to *"have"* something. At the start of a *game-series cycle,* even the *goal "To Be Godlike"* is an invented *purpose* or *game-condition*. It is a *decision* to achieve an invented *Beingness* in order to *create conditions*, or again, *"have"* something.

The *Alpha-Spirit,* to its own detriment, prefers to *have something* as opposed to *not-have something*. And in basic terms, it insists on *"having a game."* When we examine *"The Secret of Universes"* (*AT Manual #1*) narrative in relation to *games theory,* we actually find all the components of *"games"* therein. These are important to know about directly, since they are the same components we are essentially *defragmenting* with *systematic processing.* Some of these *game-conditions* include:

• *Reality-agreements* serving as *"rules"* by which we share a *game-reality* and *communication* with others that are also sharing that *reality;*

- *Implanting* (or *conditioning*) of "*rules*" that develops into one's own *postulates,* ourselves convincing ourselves of the "*rules,*" and that these are the only *rules/ games* that *can be/must be played;*

- An inherent *obedience* to the "*rules,*" and *penalties* for *disobedience* (for example, in *this Physical Universe,* "*pain*" and "*loss*");

- *Agreed-upon* (shared) "*barriers*" functioning as *limitations* imposed on *Self* and others;

- Permissible action or "*freedoms,*" which (in *game* terms) are really dependent on "*barriers*" (in order to be *free of something*);

- *Perceived value* and *sense of ownership* of "*game pieces*" representing the *player* (a "*Body*" or otherwise), and in "*slavery-enforcement games*" this includes *perceived ownership* of "*other*" *pieces/players;*

- *Complex games* include various "*levels*" of *play* being "*won,*" essentially *playing* to *win* the *"right"* to *play* more *games*, and as an "ultimate prize," the *right* to *create* *"new games"*;

• A tendency to *need* a *"new game"* created before an *"old game"* ends;

• Eventual *decay* and *deterioration* of a *game*, particularly *games* that individuals didn't fully (*knowingly*) *agree* with.

The inherent "unhappiness" found in the *Human Condition* and *Physical Universe* stems from one's inability to freely leave a *game* (*Universe*) of one's own choosing. It has become quite difficult to fully *Self-Determine* one's own relocation to another *Universe* (*game*). This *limitation* has been built into nearly all the *Penalty-Prison Universes* (see *AT Manual #1*) for quite some time.

Being "*trapped in games*" and being "*thrown out of games*" are both sources of *turbulent fragmentation* for an *Alpha-Spirit*. Yet, they continue to make *reality-agree-*

ments—or else *spiritual contracts*—with *Universes* (*games*). And as we know, at basic, the *Alpha-Spirit* is actually a quite *ethical being*. It doesn't like to "break" its own *contracts*. Therefore, having *agreed* to "*do*" something, going against this is *perceived* as a *denial-of-Self*.

---

## GOALS & PURPOSES

To assert any *individuality* (*Beingness*) within a *game*, the *Alpha-Spirit* "invents" an "*identity*." If the *game* requires "*bodies*" (as a *playing piece*), then to *play* the *game* requires using a "*Body*." We remain in *this Game*, because we don't want to "break" our *agreements*. [Isn't that nice of us?] But more recent "*incarnations*" are quite brief in duration; and we *perceive* every *entry* and *exit* point of the *game* as ourselves "making" and "breaking" *contractual agreements*. This reduces *Self-Hon-*

*esty* simply because of our previous *agreements*.

Even when we are unhappy with the *game*, we don't tend to completely *withdraw* or remove ourselves from *play*. However, we may start to *do* things that can get us expelled or exiled. Generally speaking: the *Alpha-Spirit* "*agrees*" (one way or another) to "*get in*" and then waits to be the *effect* of some other "*determinative force*" to kick them "*out.*"

When we *systematically process* "*Games and Universes*" for *Alpha-Defragmentation*, we are most concerned with "*spotting*" where the *Alpha-Spirit* is most "*at Cause.*" This means the "*entry incident*" or "*point of entry*" *into* a *game* (*Universe*). *Alpha-Defragmentation* requires a *Seeker* "*spotting*" themselves *as* the *Alpha-Spirit* (a *Beingness*) at the start of, or when entering into, *agreements* with a *game* (*Universe*). This is the only way to actually "*contact*" the *postulates* (*decisions, &tc.*) made by the individual as they *were*; not as they *are now* after innumerable *game-cycles* in *this Physical Universe*. [*AT Manual #1* is intended to assist this.]

*Goals-Implanting* occurs during each *Entry-into-a-Universe incident*, then is reinforced again during one's "*between-lives*" periods. For the *Physical Universe*, we refer to this as the "*Heaven Incident*" or "*Heaven Implant*." [See *AT Manual #1* and *PC Lesson-12*, "*Games & Universes*."]

As a result of this *implanting*, each *basic goal* an individual has gets *systematically opposed* so that there is never a true *completed-cycle* (of *action* on the *goal*). When we get "tossed out" without *ending-a-cycle*, more *attention* gets *fixed* on it —we end up with a *fixated* and *fragmented purpose*. This also means less *Actualized Awareness* is applied to the *next cycle* of *actions, goals, roles, &tc*. There is a *systematic diminishing* of *Self-Determinism* the longer we *cycle through* without ever experiencing a *creation* or *goal* manifesting as *intended.*

An individual (*Alpha-Spirit*) does have their own *actual goals* and *basic purposes;* but the *consideration* of these in *present-time* is still heavily dependent on some (previously) *implanted* and *fragmented* "*game-conditions.*" An individual *decides* on their own "*sense of purpose*" in relation to the *game;* even where it concerns basic *personality-phases* and "*roles.*" For example: "*To Be a Mother*" is to engage in the *game of* "*Being Mother*" or "*Being Motherly.*" In one's *Home Universe,* there is no necessity that such a *concept* would even *exist.*

Residual elements of *Implanted Goals* for this *Universe* (actually originating in previous *Universes*) were discovered over a century ago by *Carl Jung,* which he spoke of benignly as "*archetypes.*" And to which, the world just said "*Oh, how cute.*" Our systematic research indicates that these *"archetypes"* are a bit more significant than simply an assortment of random universal cultural ideals and icons.

As a part of *upper-level "Game-Goals Processing,"* a *Seeker* must rehabilitate their ability to *create/invent games/purposes* in the absence of *Implanted/fragmented Goals* —otherwise they are never *truly willing* to be *free* of them. When we apply *"creativeness processing"* techniques (*creating mental imagery* or *concepts*) to this area, a more effective/applicable PCL may be *"invent something..."* (rather than *"create..."*)— which does not require a physical action, but simply the systematic *"invention"* of an *"idea,"* or perhaps, *"a game."*

> Part of the resistance to "stepping out" of the *Human Condition* and *this Physical Universe* is believing that there is nowhere else *to go* and nothing else *to do*.

Remedying this is critical for successfully

"*crossing the abyss*," because an individual only "midway" across may suddenly sense that there isn't any reason *to do* anything. This is only a conditioned *fear* and *anxiety* of *dissociating* with any *personal identification* with *this Physical Universe*. It is rather like an "old cartoon" where the character can run off a ledge and defy gravity, but then falls only after they have *postulated* that there is *nothing there*.

The basis for *solidity* of any *Universe* (or *game*) is suspended in place simply by holding two *convictions* equally and simultaneously: "*that there is something there*" and "*that there is nothing there*." An individual can maintain simple *goals* without *fragmentation*. The problems occur when an *energetic-mass* (or *mental-mass*) accumulates as a result of an *Implanted-Goal* and its *Implanted-Opposition* forcefully "*colliding*."

Where a *goal* is concerned, the individual *invents* a *Beingness*, which is the "*termin-*

*al"* used *to do* that *goal.* A lot of our *frag-mentation* concerns the *"terminals"* and *"symbols"* that we *identify* with certain things. In the *"Heaven Implant,"* there is a *"terminal"* (a *"godlike being"*) representing the *Implanted-Goal "To Be Godlike."* We are then shown that *terminal* being opposed by another *terminal* (a *"free being"*) repres-enting the next goal on the *chain/series.*

This sequence immediately sets us up for *fragmentation* whenever the *Implanted-Goal "To Be Godlike"* aligns with our own *actual goal* that is being *dramatized* during a particular *cycle* of *"lifetimes."* It also sets up the *fragmentation* for the *"next person"* to be directly *opposed* to us when, for ex-ample, the *Free Being* (*terminal*) encoun-ters the *Godlike Being* (*terminal*). And as we have learned in our *systemology,* the *residual effects* of this continue to *fragment* our later *considerations* with *energetic-tur-bulence* associated with these *terminals.*

Part of our *entrapment* in *this Game* is the

*fixation* on the *Implanted-Goals*. In this case, an individual might choose one kind of *terminal* to pursue a specific *goal*; then failing at that when getting *opposed*, they will *alter* their chosen *terminal* and try again—still pursuing the same *goal*. Eventually, after several cycles of this, the *goal* becomes quite *fragmented* and essentially "*collapses*" under the weight of its accumulated *energetic-mass*; at which point the individual generally takes up the *next goal* in the *series* in an attempt to solve the problems encountered with the *first goal*. And we have all likely been through several *cycles* of the *entire sequence-chain*; but each time experiencing an even further reduction in *Self-Determinism* and *Awareness*.

One's *Actual Goals* that align with *Implanted-Goals* typically represent positive characteristics. In the "*Heaven Implant*," for example: *terminals* representing "*To Be Holy*" are *opposed* by *terminals* with the

## IMPLANTED GOAL-SEQUENCING

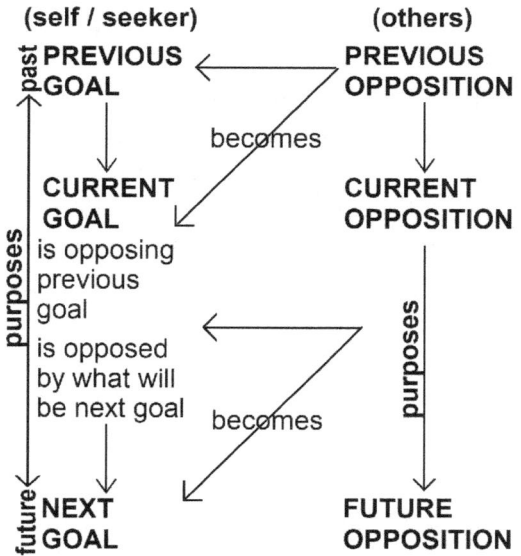

goal *"To be Intelligent."* This is the whole root of *"religion"* being *opposed by* the *"sciences"* in our world. But more importantly, the *actual* qualities of *"holiness"* and *"intelligence"* are not *"negative"*—nor are they *actually* *"opposite"* one another. The *Implant* also *fragments* the *free consideration* to be both simultaneously.

While you may uncover *"fragmented purposes"* attached to the activity previously described, it is important to note that you will *not* find a "negative goal" at the top of any cycle. The purpose of the *implanted-opposition* is because "negative goals" never *implant* directly; they are more easily rejected. Therefore, the *trap* is set to *fragment* our *actual goals*, and it relies on our resulting *fragmented considerations* to further *entrap* us. It is always our own *creations* and *postulates* that ultimately have the ability to affect us in the end.

*Alpha-Defragmentation* is intended to remove the *energetic-mass* while retaining the positive characteristics. In earlier *processing-levels*, *Beta-Defragmentation* pertained to "*spotting*" *Self* as *identified* with something or other in *this lifetime*—handling a *Seeker* as they perceive their *goals* and *roles* today. Whatever is treated at those *levels*, it does not get to the "*root*" of the *game* that we've played at for countless sequential lifetimes.

An individual's *invented purpose* or *actual intention* may not be worded exactly as found in our presentation of the "*Heaven Implant*" Goals-Sequence. For example: "*To Be a Librarian*" is not listed there; but such is a specific *terminal* with a specific *purpose*, and of which might really represent the *goal* "*To Be Intelligent*." *Running* the "*Heaven Implant*" by itself does not actually *release* you from all *goals-fragmentation*, but it does take enough "weight" off of the area in order to *spot* one's *actual goal* and how it might get *misaligned*.

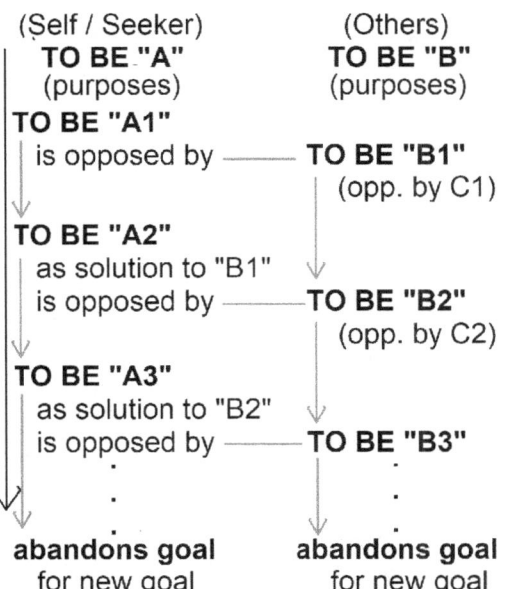

The proper *end-point* of *Systemology Level-3* (*PC Lesson-8*, *"Conquest of Illusion"*) is when a *Seeker* has *spotted* their primary *"justification consideration"* (for *this lifetime*). This is part of what an individual believes will help themselves *survive* (in the *game*) by making others wrong. What was revealed during *Level-3* may, or may not, be attached to the *actual goal* that an individual is presently *pursuing* or *dramatizing*.

The original *goal* may also have deteriorated by this point. Whatever *terminals* or *personality-phases* are treated for *this lifetime* may not be the *terminal* at the "top" of the cycle specific to their *actual goal*. This is important to determine correctly in order to *defragment* the precise *"chain"* or sequence that has brought a *Seeker* to their present state. [The point to *"spot"* is when one originally *decided* on the *actual goal*.]

A thing to remember about these *Imp-*

*lants*: *fragmented charge* on a *Goals-series* or *terminal-item* is not directly from the *Implanting-Incident* itself (which is really more of a persuasive suggestion). This is why *running* the "*incident*" itself, or an "*implant-platform*" (a list of "*command-items*"), does not provide total *defragmentation*.

The significant source of *fragmentation* is connected to *Harmful-Acts* (a *dramatization* of *fragmented purposes*) associated with our fight against others when following the pattern-sequence of the *Implanted-Goals series*.

The primary *implanted-purpose* behind *the Game* of *this Physical Universe* is "*To Survive.*" This too is at the tail end of a long sequence-chain of *goals* once attached to former *Universes* (versions of *Beta-Existence*). For example, in the "*Magic Universe,*" the primary *implanted-purpose* was/is "*To Enjoy.*"

## GOALS-BACKTRACKING BY OPPOSITION
## (EXAMPLE ONLY)

( Self )         ( Another / Others )

| TO BE INTELLIGENT | TO BE STRONG |
|---|---|

opposing previous
goal "To Be Holy"

**A Scientist**
    is opposed by . . . **A Statesman**

**A Teacher**
    is opposed by . . . **A Warlord**

**An Archaeologist**
    is opposed by . . . **A Vandal-Thief**

**A Librarian**
    is opposed by . . . **A Book-Burner**

**A Writer**
    is opposed by . . . **A Censor**

**A Critic**
goal decays
abdandoned for new goal

| TO BE STRONG |
|---|

However, in *this Physical Universe*, we find in the *"Heaven Implant"* (*entry-point*) that our *purpose* is *"To Survive"* and that this is achieved by *being* "such-and-such." And, of course, each *Implanted-Goal* (in the *series*) is attached to the primary *Games-Universe Goal*; so each is presented as equally *being* the *only* way *"To Survive."* And each is presented as both *opposing* and *being opposed by* one another. This literal *"mass of confusion"* is what sets up the *fragmented game* of *this Beta-Existence.*

---

## DEFRAGMENTING GOALS TERMINALS

Our *advanced procedure* for *"Goals Processing"* is actually a streamlined combination of *all* the techniques and methods that a *Seeker* learned and practiced during the *"Pathway to Ascension"* *Professional Course.* [That material should be kept nearby for easy reference to ensure that *systematic* use of each *process* (below) is fully understood and properly *run*.]

At this *level*—and because we have a narrow target—fewer *processes* are required of each type. [A *biofeedback device* may be used (if available) to ensure *turbulent charge* is fully *defragmented* for each *process* before *running* the next one.] The real determinant factor of success is the amount (or level) of *Actualized Awareness* and *ability-to-confront* a *Seeker* can apply to these *processing sessions*.

It is likely to take several *sessions* to complete a single pass through this *procedure* on a single *goal* (making certain to resume each *session* precisely where the last one left off). The *procedure* provides the greatest *effect* or *release* when applied to one's *actual goal*. But, it may be applied to *any goal*. In fact, an *advanced Seeker* can benefit strongly from *processing* the entire *goals-sequence* in this wise, taking each *goal* in turn.

The approximate *goal-sequencing* from the "Heaven Implant" (in descending order) is: *To Be Godlike*; *To Be Free*; *To Be Responsible*; *To Be Creative*; *To Be Important*; *To Be Competent*; *To Be Famous*; *To Be Perceptive*; *To Be Energetic*; *To Be Meticulous*; *To Be Successful*; *To Be Right (Accurate)*; *To Be Popular*; *To Be Skillful*; *To Be Wise*; *To Be Beautiful*; *To Be Productive*; *To Be Powerful*; *To Be Holy*; *To Be Intelligent*; *To Be Strong*; *To Be Crafty*; *To Be Brave*; *To Be Wealthy*; *To Be Independent*; *To Be Good*; *To Be Adventurous*; *To Be Orderly*; *To Be Different*; *To Be Respected*; *To Be Happy*; *To Be Acquisitive (Acquire)*; *To Be Sensual*; *To Be Domineering*; *To Be Tough*; and *To Be Enduring*. [The sequence cycles repeatedly from the top; *Enduring People* in *opposition* to *Godlike Beings*.]

To standardize alternating-PCL (when treating "*circuits*") for this *procedure*, the general *terminals* are: *"you"* (meaning *Self*), *"another"* (meaning specific individuals singularly), and *"others"* (meaning groups or society). The *circuits* include: *"out-flow"* (*you* projecting to *another* or *others*), *"in-flow"* (*you* receiving from *another* or *others*), and *"cross-flow"* (*you* perceiving the interaction of *others*).

This *procedure* is intended to remove enough layers of *fragmentation* whereby a *Seeker* is able to regain clearer *recall* and *understanding* of the track that led to the present. It is only when we can *"spot"* ourselves (as the *Alpha-Spirit*) as we were at the time of making various *postulates* and specific *decisions* that we are able to fully erase the effects of an *Implant*.

An *incident* or *Implant* itself is not really what we *defragment* with *systematic processing*, but instead, the *point* in which we *actually decided* (*at Cause*) to allow it to affect us—and our later *considerations* and *actions*, *&tc.*

Once enough layers of *fragmented perception/consideration* are removed, clearly "*spotting*" this *point* (with full *Awareness*) and the *actual decision/postulate* we made, is the only *systematic* way to be *free* of it. We are, in essence, taking back *control* of our *Self-Determination* once we can be certain of what *Self* has *determined*.

## SECTION 1: DEFRAGMENTATION
### (*Standard Procedure — "Goals"*)

**A** : <u>OBJECTIVE EXERCISES</u>

A *goal/purpose* deteriorates the longer an individual pursues it because they "project" (*put, place, create*) more characteristics of *opposition* into others. If the *goal* is "*To Be Intelligent,*" than they tend to *consider* others "*to be stupid*" —and will even *create conditions* where this may be proven true.

• *Go to a public place. Spot individual people and postulate the positive characteristic (or ability) of the goal into each one.* [If the goal is "*To Be Beautiful,*" then *decide* that each individual is filled with, and emanating, *beauty* and *imagine* them as "*being beautiful.*"]

• *Go to a public place. Spot individual people and spot some remaining bit of the positive characteristic (or ability) in each one; validate (acknowledge) it is there and encourage it.* [This is done by *intention (telepathically)* and does not require verbal communication. The positive characteristic is a basic goal of *Beingness* in this *game* and it is present in everyone, however decayed it may now appear. Recognize this *spark* that remains present and direct your *attention/intention* to complete the exercise.]

**B** : <u>POSITIVE RECALL</u>

*Attention* on the positive (or pleasurable) characteristic of something tends to assist with handling or *confronting* the upsets and difficulties that represent its negative side. We are most *"at Cause"* when first *deciding* on a *goal*, or when initially experiencing its upper-level manifestation before it deteriorated. *Spotting* these *points* helps improve *processing* the "other side" of things—assisting one to handle *turbulence* in later *processes*. Note that if the *goal* has strongly decayed, these *points* may not be found within the present lifetime. [Insert the *ability (intelligence, beauty, &tc.)* into the PCL.]

1. *"Recall being ___."*
2. *"Recall another being ___."*
3. *"Recall others being ___."*

## C : RECALL (FLOW-FACTORS)

This is an extension of the previous step, with *four* similar *processes* involving the *"Flow-Factors"*—see *PC Lesson-7, "Eliminating Barriers."* Each *process* (of six alternating-PCL) is *run* separately. Using these various *circuits* and *factors* helps a *Seeker* get an "exterior viewpoint" on the *goals* and *terminals.* [Insert a *terminal* representing the *goal (an intelligent person, a beautiful person, &tc.)* into the PCL.]

Communication Process

1. *"Recall a time you were in good communication with a(n) ___."*

2. *"Recall a time a(n) ___ was in good communication with you."*

3. *"Recall a time another was in good communication with a(n) ___."*

4. *"Recall a time a(n) ___ was in good communication with another."*

5. *"Recall a time others were in good communication with a(n) ___."*

6. *"Recall a time a(n) ___ was in good communication with others."*

Likingness Process

1. *"Recall a time you liked a(n) ___."*

2. *"Recall a time a(n) ___ liked you."*

3. *"Recall a time another liked a(n) ___."*

4. *"Recall a time a(n) ___ liked another."*

5. *"Recall a time others liked a(n) ___."*

6. *"Recall a time a(n) ___ liked others."*

Agreement Process

1. *"Recall a time you agreed with a(n) ___."*

2. *"Recall a time a(n) ___ agreed with you."*

3. *"Recall a time another agreed with a(n) ___."*

4. *"Recall a time a(n) ___ agreed with another."*

5. *"Recall a time others agreed with a(n) ___."*

6. *"Recall a time a(n) ___ agreed with others."*

## Understanding Process

1. *"Recall a time you understood a(n) ___."*

2. *"Recall a time a(n) ___ understood you."*

3. *"Recall a time another understood a(n) ___."*

4. *"Recall a time a(n) ___ understood another."*

5. *"Recall a time others understood a(n) ___."*

6. *"Recall a time a(n) ___ understood others."*

## D : UNDERSTANDING

*Defragmenting "communication-flows" as-*

sists a *Seeker* in "*eliminating barriers*" of *existence*. For this *process*, focus on positive interaction. Effectiveness of this is found in sheer quantity. *Imagine* "saying" many things, about anything, so long as there is a *flow*. [These are alternating-PCL using a *terminal*.]

1. "*Imagine saying specific things to a(n) ___.*"

2. "*Imagine a(n) ___ saying specific things to you.*"

3. "*Imagine another saying specific things to a(n) ___.*"

4. "*Imagine a(n) ___ saying specific things to another.*"

5. "*Imagine others saying specific things to a(n) ___.*"

6. "*Imagine a(n) ___ saying specific things to others.*"

**E** : <u>HELP</u>

Accumulated "*failure*" to *help others* contributes to deterioration of a *goal*. We are conditioned to take *"failure"* very seriously—and too often it is *perceived* to "outweigh" those times when we were *successful* at *helping others*. If a present *goal* has heavily *"collapsed"* (at the end of its cycle), then an individual must *spot* the *successes* much earlier on the *Backtrack.* If that *recall* isn't accessible, even the smallest *successes* in *this lifetime* may be *recalled* in place of the earlier positive activity that has not yet *resurfaced*.

1. *"Recall a time you helped a(n) ___."*
2. *"Recall a time a(n) ___ helped you."*
3. *"Recall a time another helped a(n) ___."*
4. *"Recall a time a(n) ___ helped another."*
5. *"Recall a time others helped a(n) ___."*
6. *"Recall a time a(n) ___ helped others."*

**F** : <u>PROTECTING</u>

This is an extension of the previous step. *Fragmentation* connected to *"failure to protect"* is similar to, but tends to be more *turbulent* than, *"failure to help."* The concepts of *"love and loss"* and *"trust and betrayal"* also fall under this category. The negative side of these areas cannot be *processed-out* using *"basic analytical recall"* directly. That just validates the negative misemotion. However, *basic recall* may be used to validate the positive *"successful"* side (increasing one's *Awareness*) prior to treating anything more *turbulent*.

1. *"Recall a time you protected a(n) ___."*
2. *"Recall a time a(n) ___ protected you."*
3. *"Recall a time another protected a(n) ___."*
4. *"Recall a time a(n) ___ protected another."*
5. *"Recall a time others protected a(n) ___."*
6. *"Recall a time a(n) ___ protected others."*

## G : PROBLEMS/SOLUTIONS

When an individual *solves* a *problem*, they tend to treat that *solution* as an *absolute*. It becomes *The Solution* to all, even when it no longer really applies or is relevant. Unfortunately, living this way only gets the person into more *problems*. And as the *"old solution"* continues being applied (and *failing*), these *problems* tend to stack up (as accumulated *imprinting*).

The same pattern is found in deterioration of a *goals-chain*. An individual starts off with a particular *goal* at the top of whatever cycle it happens to be; and when meeting opposition, that *goal* is *altered* in order to sustain it, until it is *perceived* as no longer sustainable. Each of those *alterations* were *"solutions"* to a specific *"problem,"* yet they remained on the *chain* thereafter, serving to affect the *consideration* of future *terminals* used for the *goal*.

In brief: after *opposition* occurs, and we *alter* our *character* to *solve* a "present" *problem*, we never return to the point of when we originally had the *goal*. The *alterations* are kept in place to continue to *solve* whatever future *problems* occur; and *failing* in that, additional layers of *alteration* are then added sequentially, but never removed. This is what we consider *fragmentation*. And this is how a *goal* decays.

The technique applied here requires *spotting a problem*, and then *spotting solutions* (one, or as many as easily come up); then *spot another problem* and its *solutions*, and so on. Ideally, a *Seeker* will *spot* earlier and earlier *problems* on the *Backtrack*, and also *solutions* that are still held in place, but no longer appropriate. It is okay if *attention* returns to more recent *problems/solutions* in between. Just keep handling whatever comes up to a satisfactory *endpoint* of "feeling better" (or "clearer") about the *terminal* and its *goal*.

This practice is intricate enough that each *circuit-flow* (pair of PCL) is best *run* as its own *process*. [For *Solo-Piloting*: repeat the *solutions*-PCL as many times as necessary for a single *problem*. For *Co-Piloting*: alternate the PCL.]

1A. *"What problem might a(n) ___ have with another or others?"*

1B. *"What solutions might a(n) ___ have to that problem?"*

2A. *"What problem might another (or others) have with a(n) ___?"*

2B. *"What solutions might they have to that problem?"*

3A. *"What problem might a(n) ___ observe between others?"*

3B. *"What solution might a(n) ___ have to their problem?"*

4A. *"What problem might a(n) ___ create for themselves?"*

4B. *"What solutions might a(n) ___ have to that problem?"*

**H** : <u>HARMFUL-ACTS/HOLD-BACKS</u>

Here we directly *process* the *Seeker* "at Cause." An individual will *do* things, then hide what's been done, and gradually *withdraw* from the related area. It doesn't matter whether it was from *ill-intention* or the *best of intention gone wrong*. Eventually, this *fragmentation* accumulates to a point where the individual *holds-back* from *doing* things, and *holds-out* on *communication* and *contact* with their *environment—others, Universe, &tc.*

This *processing* technique simply requires a *Seeker* actually *confront* what they *have done.* This is an important part of regaining the *"responsibility" for "doing"* things —which is how we regain *"ability"* to *"do"* things. Here we are only concerned with the *doingness*; not any *ethical judgments.* This technique does not even require that the *"done"* things be *Harmful-Acts.*

*Harmful-Acts* are the primary target of the technique, but this area shouldn't be forced or pushed in any way. They should naturally *resurface* as a part of the *processing.*

Our desirable *goals* often become *fragmented* in such a way that maintaining them and *solving a problem* or *resolving a confusion* has caused us to act with "*ill-intent.*" These "fixed ideas" we establish for handling *problems* and *confusions* develop into compulsive "*fixated purposes.*" However, many promising *Seekers* have "spun in to oblivion" by placing too much emphasis and attention on directly uncovering "*evil intentions.*"

As with the previous step, each *circuit-flow* (pair of PCL) is best *run* as its own *process.* The alternating-PCL target *doingness* and *hold-backs.* We use the word "*might*" to allow a wider range of *consideration*, and also so a *Seeker* does not feel "attacked"—as with the more direct PCL: "*What have you done?*" [For *Alpha-Defragmentation*: this technique is quite useful for also treating *oppositional terminals* of *future-goals* and *past-goals* during later applications of this *Standard Procedure for Goals*.]

1A. *"What might a(n) ___ do to another?"*

1B. *"What might a(n) ___ hold-back from another?"*

2A. *"What might another do to a(n) ___?"*

2B. *"What might another hold-back from a(n) ___?"*

3A. *"What might a(n) ___ do to others?"*

3B. *"What might a(n) ___ hold-back from others?"*

4A. *"What might a(n) ___ do to themselves?"*

4B. *"What might a(n) ___ hold-back from themselves?"*

5A. *"What might you do to a(n) ___?"*

5B. *"What might you hold-back from a(n) ___?"*

# I : <u>CHANGE</u>

If an individual is *unwilling* to *change*, then they can't improve. *"Getting better"* is a *change* in *condition*. Both *insistence on*, and *resistance to*, "change," is *fragmentation*. It inspires *harmful-acts* and incites *upsets* and *problems* between individuals.

Generally speaking, the *"identities"* (*role-terminals*) we use (that are attached to our *goals-chain*) are chosen as a *fixed solution* to a specific *perceived "problem of livingness."* An individual is *resistant to* changing *fixed ideas*, even when doing so would provide a better *"condition of livingness."* [*Run* these *processes* like the previous step.]

1A. *"What might a(n) ___ want to change about another?"*

1B. *"What might a(n) ___ prevent changing about another?"*

2A. *"What might another want to change about a(n) ___?"*

2B. *"What might another prevent changing about a(n) ___?"*

3A. *"What might a(n) ___ want to change about others?"*

3B. *"What might a(n) ___ prevent changing about others?"*

4A. *"What might a(n) ___ want to change about themselves?"*

4B. *"What might a(n) ___ prevent changing about themselves?"*

5A. *"What might you want to change about a(n) ___?"*

5B. *"What might you prevent changing about a(n) ___?"*

## J : <u>UPSETS (FLOW-FACTOR BREAKS)</u>

Personal *turbulence* (and *upsets* between *terminals*) happens whenever one of the *flow-factors*—*communication, likingness,* and *agreement*—are either *"inhibited"* or *"enforced."* And, since *Buddha* so aptly stated that *"all suffering comes from desire,"* we may as well add *"desire"* [*"desired"*] to this list of "buttons" too. [To clarify for *upper-level processing*: by *"agreement,"* we also mean *"reality."*]

When a *"break"* in a *flow* occurs, the *"reaction"* is generally more extreme (turbulent) than the situation calls for. This is due to accumulated *fragmentation* of the *flow* (from many *earlier similar incidents*). For *systematic processing*: when a *Seeker* *"spots"* the moment they became *upset* and the exact *flow-factors* involved, some relief is gained. If they can work back to *"spotting"* earlier *upsets* of the same *flow-factors*, an increased level of *Awareness* and *ability-to-confront* is gained for that area. [Complete *Alpha-Defragmentation* occurs from *"spotting"* the *earliest* time or very first incident (presumably in other *lifetimes* in other *Universes*). To treat *"Home Universe"* (or prior), *"not-know"* would be required on the list of "buttons."]

For this procedure: we are not *processing* a specific *upset*, but instead are treating all of the *flow-factors* with a specific *terminal*. Each *process* consists of *five* alternating-PCL. Ideally, a *Seeker* will uncover "earlier" or "deeper" data as they cycle through the PCL repeatedly for a single *process*.

Communication — Inhibited

1. *"What communication might a(n) ___ inhibit in another?"*

2. *"What communication might another inhibit in a(n) ___?"*

3. *"What communication might a(n) ___ inhibit in others?"*

4. *"What communication might a(n) ___ inhibit themselves from saying?"*

5. *"What communication might you inhibit a(n) ___ from saying?"*

Communication — Enforced

1. *"What communication might a(n) ___ enforce on another?"*

2. *"What communication might another enforce on a(n) ___?"*

3. *"What communication might a(n) ___ enforce on others?"*

4. *"What communication might a(n) ___ force on themselves?"*

5. *"What communication might you force on a(n) ___?"*

Communication—Desired

1. *"What communication might a(n) ___ desire from another?"*

2. *"What communication might another desire from a(n) ___?"*

3. *"What communication might a(n) ___ desire from others?"*

4. *"What communication might a(n) ___ make themselves desire?"*

5. *"What communication might you desire from a(n) ___?"*

Likingness—Inhibited

1. *"What might a(n) ___ inhibit another from liking?"*

2. *"What might another inhibit a(n) ___ from liking?"*

3. *"What might a(n) ___ inhibit others from liking?"*

4. *"What might a(n) ___ inhibit themselves from liking?"*

5. *"What might you inhibit a(n) ___ from liking?"*

Likingness—Enforced

1. *"What might a(n) ___ enforce another to like?"*

2. *"What might another enforce a(n) ___ to like?"*

3. *"What might a(n) ___ enforce others to like?"*

4. *"What might a(n) ___ force themselves to like?"*

5. *"What might you force a(n) ___ to like?"*

Likingness—Desired

1. *"What likingness might a(n) ___ desire from another?"*

2. *"What likingness might another desire from a(n) ___?"*

3. *"What likingness might a(n) ___ desire from others?"*

4. *"What likingness might a(n) ___ make themselves desire?"*

5. *"What likingness might you desire from a(n) ___?"*

Agreement—Inhibited/Rejected

1. *"What agreement might a(n) ___ reject from another?"*

2. *"What agreement might another reject from a(n) ___?"*

3. *"What agreement might a(n) ___ reject from others?"*

4. *"What agreement might a(n) ___ make themselves reject?"*

5. *"What agreement might you reject from a(n) ___ ?"*

Agreement—Enforced

1. *"What agreement might a(n) ___ enforce on another?"*

2. *"What agreement might another enforce on a(n) ___ ?"*

3. *"What agreement might a(n) ___ enforce on others?"*

4. *"What agreement might a(n) ___ force on themselves?"*

5. *"What agreement might you force on a(n) ___ ?"*

Agreement—Desired

1. *"What agreement might a(n) ___ desire from another?"*

2. *"What agreement might another desire from a(n) ___ ?"*

3. *"What agreement might a(n) ___ desire from others?"*

4. *"What agreement might a(n) ___ make themselves desire?"*

5. *"What agreement might you desire from a(n) ___ ?"*

**K** : <u>JUSTIFICATION CONSIDERATIONS</u>

*The Game* of *this Physical Universe* is *"To*

*Survive."* Unfortunately, most of an individual's *considerations*, *thought-activity*, and *actions*, all stem from this premise. While *fixedly trapped* in *considerations "To Survive,"* an individual will allow themselves to commit *harmful-acts* and then bury their memory and responsibility under heavy layers of *fragmented justification.*

The following *process* contains *four* PCL that are cycled repeatedly; however, several *"B-responses"* may be derived from each *"A-question."* All *four* PCL should be run in *series* as a single *process*.

1A. *"What would a(n) ___ do to ensure their survival?"*

1B. *"What justifications would they have for that?"*

2A. *"What would a(n) ___ stop others from doing, to ensure their own survival?"*

2B. *"What justifications would they have for that?"*

We want to *defragment* the precise *consideration* that is used to *justify*/make others wrong. To find this, we *defragment* some of the "possible" *considerations* on that line before selecting one to *process*. [These alternating-PCL are run repetitively.]

1. *"How might a(n) ___ make themselves right?"*

2. *"How might a(n) ___ make others wrong?"*

The next *processing*-PCL for this procedure is more direct and it requires listing-out answers; but the intent is finding *a specific answer*. The direct PCL is:

*"What would a(n) ___ use to make others wrong?"*

By this, we generally mean an "excuse" (or *justification*) in the form of a *"They're all..."* or *"Everyone else is..."* answer. Ideally, this type of listing technique would be performed using a *biofeedback device* in order to *spot* the answer that *"reads"* on a *GSR-Meter*. Alternative directions for this *process* are found in *PC Lesson-8*. [Unlike its treatment in *Systemology Level-3*, we do not restrict this PCL to *"In this lifetime."*] If the above PCL *does not* produce the *basic answer* in the style-form described, list from the following:

*"From the viewpoint of a(n) \_\_\_, what is it about people that makes them so wrong?"*

Using the most correct *basic answer* found, *run* the following alternating-PCL. The *end-point* should include *defragmentation* of any *fixed* or *turbulent considerations* connected with the *goals-terminal*. [Even when it is not a *Seeker's present-goal* or *actual-goal*, there is usually some *energetic-mass* "entangled" with the *justification considerations* of *terminals* for other *goals*.]

1. *"How would {answer} make others wrong?"*

2. *"How would {answer} make a(n) \_\_\_ right?"*

## L : EXTERIOR VIEWPOINTS

Ultimately, the *processing-goal* is for a *Seeker* to get *"exterior to"* the *energetic-mass* or *fixed condition* that they are compulsively *"inside of"* (as a *viewpoint*). *Fragmentation* is best handled from *"the outside."* As a final step to Section-1, *run the following PCL in cycles to a satisfactory end-point.*

1. *"From where could you communicate to a(n) ___ ?"*

2. *"From where could a(n) ___ communicate to you?"*

3. *"From where could a(n) ___ communicate to others?"*

4. *"From where could a(n) ___ communicate to themselves?"*

## SECTION 2: GOAL-SEQUENCING
(*For defrag and research processing*)

*Advanced Training* materials—our *upper-level Ascension Technology*—resulted from many years of experimental *research-processing*. This was conducted by *Self-Honest* individuals that had completed our earliest presentations of *Beta-Defragmentation Procedure*. [Referring to the *Systemology Core Research Volumes*.]

Some of these *research-methods* run parallel with workable *defragmentation-methods,* as given in these next two sections. [*Biofeedback Devices* were also used to compile data from each *Seeker* that could then be comparatively examined in relation to additional research from "outside sources."]

Advisement: the *Implanted Goal-Sequence* of the *"Heaven Incident"* is only a *strongly implanted suggestion*; a *Seeker's* own *"sequence"* may differ slightly. [Hence we use this standard procedure for *Level-7 processing.*]

**A** : <u>BASIC OPPOSITION</u>

Once a *goal-terminal* is *defragmented* with Section-1, sufficient *charge* will also have been taken off *considerations* of an *oppositional goal-terminal* so that it can be *processed* directly. For every *goal-terminal*, there will be a *basic opposite* to it. For example: for the *goal "To Be Intelligent,"* the *basic opposite* (as a *terminal*) is *"stupid people"* or *"a stupid person."*

Because the *Implanted Goal-Sequencing* is patterned the way it is, there is technically *"opposition"* on *"both sides"* of an *Implanted Goal.* By this we mean both the *previous-goal* and the *next-goal* in the *sequence.* We want to *spot* the *characteristic* of the *basic opposite* for the present *goal*—such as *"a stupid person."*

It is only due to *fragmentation* that its *consideration* is applied to *terminals* representing a *former* or *future sequential-goal*; in this example, associating the *characteristic* of *"stupidity"* with *"To Be Strong"* (*next goal*) and/or *"To Be Holy"* (*previous goal*). [Any *fragmented cross-consideration* of this kind connected to *Implanted Goals* must be *processed-out* for total *Alpha-Defragmentation*.]

To be systematic, the direct PCL for producing the *basic opposite* requires *listing* (most of Section-2 does), preferably with a *biofeedback device*.

*"What type of people would a(n) ___ oppose?"*

If this isn't listed properly, it can result in misappropriating the *characteristic* on the *previous goal-terminal*; such as *"stupid holy people."* If the above PCL *does not* produce the *basic opposite*, list from the following (but being certain not to misappropriate the *characteristic* onto the *next goal-terminal*, such as *"stupid strong people"*):

*"What type of people would a(n) ____ be opposed by?"*

If neither PCL seems to produce a *basic answer* directly, look for a common characteristic between the two lists; in this example, again, *"stupid people."*

**B** : <u>OPPOSITION TERMINAL</u>

The original *goal-terminal* and its *basic opposition* (from Step-A) are used for this *process*. The PCL is printed here with the words *"terminal"* and *"opposition"* appearing in *brackets*. In the example we have been using: *"an intelligent person"* or *"intelligent people"* is the *goal-terminal*; and *"a stupid person"* or *"stupid people"* is the *opposition*. This *series* of *eight* PCL are cycled to a satisfactory *end-point*.

1. *"What action or attitude would {opposition} have towards {terminal}?"*

2. *"What action or attitude would {terminal} have towards {opposition}?"*

3. *"What action or attitude would {terminal} have towards others?"*

4. *"What action or attitude would others have towards {terminal}?"*

5. *"What action or attitude would {opposition} have towards others?"*

6. *"What action or attitude would others have towards {opposition}?"*

7. *"What action or attitude would {opposition} hold-back from {terminal}?"*

8. *"What action or attitude would {terminal} hold-back from {opposition}?"*

## C : <u>FINDING THE NEXT GOAL</u>

Because a *Seeker* generally works *"back-wards"* up the *goals-chain* that has led to the present, when a *previous goal* is *run*, the later one (*current goal*) has already been handled. But, when *running* the *"current"* goal, you might not know what the *next/future* goal is going to be. Of course, this might be obvious as a result of previous *processing*, or from the *Implanted Goal-Sequencing* (from the "*Heaven Implant*")—but the *Goal-Sequence* in that *Implant* is only a "strong suggestion" or "guideline" that sets up a *pattern*. This means your own actual *goals-postulates* may differ slightly from that exact *sequence*.

Within each primary *goal*, there is also a *chain* of its deterioration. This is how we cycle from one *goal* to the next over the course of various lifetimes; starting up "at the top" of a *goal* with full vigor, and then moving "downward" as we struggle with it and *alter* it in the face of *opposition*. Usually "at the top" there is not much contact with *opposition* or the *next goal* of the *sequence*. In that case, you might skip over treating it since there is no real *turbulence* to *process-out*. But, if you are already going "out the bottom" of your *current goal*, then there may already be some serious *harmful-acts* and *hold-backs* stacking up on the *next goal.*

This *listing*-PCL is:

*"What goal would successfully oppose the {current goal}?"*

This could be restated in many ways. You could also word it to *list* for the *next oppositional terminal* as:

*"What type of person would successfully oppose a(n) {current goal terminal}?"*

 –or–

*"What type of person would be dangerous to a(n) \_\_\_?"*

Once you have *The Goal* (or a *basic characteristic*), you can find that *basic goal-terminal* by *listing*:

*"Who or what would want {goal}?"*

If you have a *terminal,* you can verify the *basic goal* by *listing*:

*"What goal would a(n) \_\_\_ have?"*

To ascertain one's own *goal-sequencing*, a *Seeker* will work around a bit, using a number of these types of PCL (such as given here in Section-2) until they are satisfied that answers all logically fit together. [This is all not as complicated to handle as it might seem at first glace, it is simply a very systematic way to recover precise data for *processing* precise targets.]

When you have finished this step, a *Seeker* should have discovered the *next goal* and its *terminal* (which is the *future oppositional terminal* of the *current goal*). It may be that there is no *future oppositional terminal* in view yet. [When handling *earlier/previous goals*, you will already know the answers to these PCL, so you simply use steps such as this (with a *biofeedback device*, if available) to check over the data and make sure it is correct.]

**D** : <u>FUTURE OPPOSITION (TERMINAL)</u>

For this part, use the same *process* given

in Step-B. This time, insert the *future oppositional terminal* in the "*{opposition}*" bracket. When handling one's actual *current-goal*, there may not be much *turbulent fragmentation* connected to this area.

However, if a *Seeker* is nearing an *end-cycle* on their *current goal*, there will often be many *hold-backs* and *harmful-acts* against what represents the next "*goals-package*" that is in a *Seeker's future.* [If it seems necessary, other *processes* (such as those in the *PC lessons*, of which Section-1 is based on) may be applied to reduce the *turbulence.*]

When using a *biofeedback device*: there is a phenomenon where the "*needle*" of a *GSR-Meter* may behave *violently* or *turbulently*—and even "*slam*" against the "*posts*" at either end. Assuming this is not caused by a *Seeker* wearing something *metallic* (like a *ring*)—or touching/shorting *two electrodes* together (which you shouldn't do)—this *usually* means a *term-*

*inal* (or *area*) has been *contacted* (*in processing*) that a *Seeker* has significant *harmful-act/hold-outs* (*fragmentation*) stacked up against.

When not using a *biofeedback device*: the indicator for the same (above) is an increased sense of *"hatred"* or *"evil intent"* toward the *future oppositional terminal*. This same indicator may be found in regard to one's own *current-goal* or *previous-goals* or really any *area* that is treated in *processing*.

In either case: a *Seeker* should *spot* the earlier *"evil intentions"* and *"fragmented purposes,"* and simply *defragment-by-inspection* (by one's own *Awareness*). Full *defragmentation* only occurs by *spotting* the *earliest* such *incident* on the *chain*. [While this matter must be handled properly, we do not encourage "scouting" for various *evil intentions* and *fragmented purposes* that are not directly a part of the area being treated.]

When an individual is *processing* their own *previous-goals*: much of the information about a *"future goal"* will already be known, or have been handled, since the *Seeker* is working/*processing* through their own personal *sequence* "backwards" — quite literally, *"backtracking."* But if there is any remaining *turbulence* attached to a *"future goal"* (relative to whatever *goal* is being treated as *"current,"* but only as a *viewpoint* for *processing purposes*), then it may be handled further with alternating-PCL:

1. *"What would {goal-terminal} do to {future oppositional terminal}?"*

2. *"What would {goal-terminal} hold-back from {future oppositional terminal}?"*

## E : FINDING THE PREVIOUS GOAL

Next, we want to find the *goal* that came before whatever one is being treated/*processed* (as *"current"*). Note that the *"problems"* of the *previous goal* are *"solved"* by the *"current"* goal. The procedure for this is like Step-C, except this time you are looking backwards. This means, how the *"current"* goal is *opposing* a *"previous"* goal. Here we want to determine *what* the *goal* is that the *"current"* goal is *opposing*.

This *listing*-PCL is:

*"What goal would be successfully opposed by the {current goal}?"*

You can reword it to *list* for the *prior oppositional terminal* as:

*"What type of person would be successfully opposed by a(n) {current goal terminal}?"*

## F : PREVIOUS OPPOSITION (TERMINAL)

For *processing* the *oppositional terminal* to the *previous-goal* (using the perspective or *viewpoint* of the *previous goal* as "current"), apply the *process* from Step-B. This time, insert the *previous oppositional terminal* in the "*{opposition}*" bracket.

When handling one's actual *current-goal*,

a *recall* of significant *harmful-acts* may *re-surface*—those which a *Seeker* committed when they were actually on the *previous goal*. To defragment this, *run*:

1. *"What harmful act might {goal-terminal} do against {previous oppositional terminal}?"*

2. *"How would they justify that?"*

If what *resurfaces* only generates additional *turbulence* (*GSR-Meter* "slams" or feelings of ill-intention) and does not improve significantly with the above PCL, a *Seeker* may also have to *"spot"* the instances of *"evil intention"* or *"fragmented purpose"* earlier on the *chain* to really get *"free"* of it.

While the full Section-2 procedure may require a bit of practice, once a *Seeker* is *"flying"* on it, the *energetic-mass* of the *Goals-Sequence* starts unraveling quite quickly. Having completed the procedure on a *Seeker's* own actual *"current goal,"* there should be a greater *Awareness* of the abandoned *"previous goal."* Following along this *pattern*, further *backward*, a *Seeker* may be able to more easily "plot" more of their own *Backtrack*.

When a *Seeker* has completed this procedure on a *"current goal,"* it may then be repeated for *running* the *next previous goal* (which was identified above). Alternatively, a *Seeker* may continue to Section-3 using the data for whatever is being treated as *"current goal."*

# SECTION 3: OBJECT-ITEMS/ SYMBOLS
## (*For defrag and research processing*)

*Terminals* are *masses*. They are "things" at the other end of our *attention-flow*. Most often, *terminals* represent specific individuals, or types of people, handled as "*circuits*" in our *processes*. But other "living things" are also *terminals*—such as *animals* or even *trees*.

Inanimate mass—"*physical objects*"—are also *terminals*. While we may use "*objects*" in earlier *processing-levels* as a focus of *attention* in many "*objective exercises*," we do not actually *run processes* on their "significance" until here at *Level-7*. Even now, we are only concerned with certain types of "*object-items*."

As the narrative in *AT Manual #1* suggests: to an *Alpha-Spirit*, "*symbols*" relay a level of strong *communication* that is very *real*, but much more subtle than what *standard-issue Humans* are likely to *perceive* directly in their everyday lives. [*Processing-out* the *fragmented significance* attached to a *"basic goal object-item"* should only be handled *after* the *goal* itself has been treated with the procedures in Section-1 and Section-2.]

**A** : <u>BASIC OBJECT-ITEM (SYMBOL)</u>

There is a *"basic object-item"* that represents, or more accurately, *"symbolizes"* a single *goal-chain* (which includes all the times the same *goal* was *altered* to meet *opposition*, before the individual changed their *goals* completely). Some version of this *"object"* is likely to be present (even literally carried or worn) during one's entire time with the *goal*. This may or may not be the same *"symbol"* (*object*) that was used to represent the *goal* during an *Implanting-Incident*.

The *"basic object"* we are referring to here

acts very much like a *"basic brick"* when an individual *constructs* their foundation for a *goal*. The individual may use it as a *"substitute"* for themselves, or like a *"playing piece"* (similar to the way players of the *"Monopoly"* *board-game* represent themselves with arbitrary "objects").

For example: the *intelligent-person* might always have a *book*; an *acquisitive-person* might always have a *camera*; the *beautiful-person* might always have a *hairbrush* or *mirror*; and so on. These are only examples. And they are not necessarily identical to all individuals operating with a certain *goal*. Section-3 is applied to make certain of this *"basic object"* and then *defragment* some of the *charge* attached to it.

At an *upper-level* of existence—due to *Implanting* and *mental-machinery*—the *Alpha-Spirit* keeps a version of the *"basic goal object-item"* *compulsively created* in a space that is outside (or *"exterior to"*) this *Physi-*

*cal Universe.* All *communications* relayed from the *Alpha-Spirit* to this *Beta-Existence* (down the *ZU-Line* to the *"Physical Body"*) are passing *"through"* this *object-item*. We apparently also use it for *memory storage*.

This *basic object* is intentionally "hidden" and "forgotten" out of *fear* that someone else might *"read their mind"* and *"zap it"* and thus *"destroy"* their *communication-line* with this *existence*. In some ways the individual uses this as a sort of *"Spiritual Body"* for the lifespan of the *goal*. The only *active item* being used is attached to a *Seeker's* actual *"current goal"* —but there is likely *fragmentation* and *restimulative-potential* still imprinted with other previously used *"basic goal object-items."*

Either the *goal* or a *terminal* (for the *goal*) may be used for the *listing*-PCL:

*"What object-item would represent ___?"*

For example: *"a strong person"* or *"the goal, To Be Strong."* Additional instruction:

whatever is *identified* as *"The Object-Item,"* insert it in the *blank space* for remaining PCL (below) in Section-3.

## B : <u>PLEASING PEOPLE/ADMIRATION</u>

It has been found that an individual has the tendency to use the *"object-item"* as a *"people-pleaser."* They may *create it,* or put it up, in place of themselves so as to *attract admiration, &tc.* [A more obvious illustrative example of this is the *"statue"* a *"god-like being"* might use as substitute for their own actual presence.]

1. *"What sort of ___ would please people?"*

2. *"What type of person would that please?"*

After *processing* those *considerations,* apply the following series of alternating-PCL as a single *process:*

1. *"Spot a time someone admired your ___."*

2. *"Spot a time someone invalidated your ___."*

3. *"Spot a time you admired someone's ___."*

4. *"Spot a time you invalidated someone's ___."*

Then practice this next exercise until you feel good about *processing* the *object-item* further.

*"Imagine crowds of cheering people, applauding, and admiring the ___."*

## C : HELP

Increased attachment to the "object-item" results from an individual using it *"To Survive"* (the upper-most governing *Game-Goal* of *this Physical Universe*). *Run* the following *five* alternating-PCL as a single *process* until all of the presently available *considerations* are *spotted*.

1. *"How could a ___ help you?"*
2. *"How could you help a ___?"*
3. *"How could a ___ help another?"*
4. *"How could another help a ___?"*
5. *"How could a ___ help itself?"*

## D : PROTECTING

That this *"object-item"* can be lost, dam-aged, or destroyed, is a constant source of *anxiety* and *fear. Run* the following *process* like the previous step.

1. *"How could a ___ protect you?"*

2. *"How could you protect a ___?"*

3. *"How could a ___ protect another?"*

4. *"How could another protect a ___?"*

5. *"How could a ___ protect itself?"*

## E : RESISTANCE/STOPPED MOTION

This *"object-item"* tends to "stop" *motion* and *activity* in some way. Its *presence/ex-istence* may also be *resisted* by others. In either case, *Awareness* is "suspended" and the *"object-item"* accumulates further *en-ergetic-mass. Run* each of the next *two* PCL-*series* (below) as separate *processes*.

1. *"What motion or activity of yours has a ___ stopped?"*

2. *"What motion or activity of someone else has a ___ stopped?"*

3. *"What motion or activity of others has a ___ stopped?"*

1. *"What beingness (or type of being) would resist a ___?"*

2. *"What beingness (or type of being) would ___ resist?"*

**F** : <u>OBJECTIVE EXERCISE</u>

For this exercise you will need a physical representation of the *object-item*. If treating your *actual "current-goal"* then you may already have a *physical copy* of this *object-item* in your possession. If you are treating the immediately *previous goal* to your *actual current-goal*, then such representations were likely abandoned long ago (in which case you will either have to get one or make one). The critical part of this exercise is having the *"physical mass"* present.

Place the *object-item* at least a foot out in

front of you, or on a table. This is a physical exercise requiring you to intentionally reach for the item and then let go of it. You want to be able to move your arm at least a foot or so—as a deliberate action—for each part. *Run* the following *series* of *six* PCL as a single repetitive *process*.

1A. *"Grab the object and intend to 'keep it from going away'."*

1B. *"Let go of it."*

2A. *"Grab the object and intend to 'hold it absolutely still'."*

2B. *"Let go of it."*

3A. *"Grab the object and intend to 'make it more solid'."*

3B. *"Let go of it."*

**G** : <u>WASTING EXERCISE</u>

Part of any *compulsive creation* (or *fixed consideration*) is the inability to "let go" (or have a change in condition). The *con-*

*siderations* (and *perceived significance*) attached to an *"object-item"* are what makes the "loss" so *emotionally fragmenting,* or cause us to *fix* a lot of our *attention* on it to prevent this. The following exercise is intended to help *defragment* these *considerations.* Each PCL (below) should be *run* repeatedly as its own *process.* [By "waste," we mean to *dispense with, use up, destroy, &tc.*—meaning the opposite of *having, keeping,* or *accumulating.* You may need to insert a *plural* form of the *object-item.*]

1. *"Imagine a way to waste ___."*

2. *"Imagine a way for another to waste ___."*

3. *"Imagine a way for others to waste ___."*

**H** : HAVING EXERCISE

This technique requires practice with the *"creativeness"*-style techniques found throughout previous *processing-levels.* The following steps are treated as a single *process* or exercise.

• *Imagine great quantities of the object-item in a sphere surrounding you.*

• *Continue making copies, but making them more and more deteriorated or decayed. Keep changing their colors so that they are knowingly under your control as your creations (and not copies of a compulsively created image).*

• *Imagine/create more and more copies of them in the surrounding sphere until they start flowing-in on the Body. If you need to give them a gentle 'push in' to the Body, you may; but never from an interior viewpoint of 'pulling in' to the Body.*

• *Continue this until you feel comfortable 'throwing some away' (similar to 'wasting').*

• *Imagine/create more copies and have them 'out-flow' into the distance slowly disappearing; and then 'out-flow' more into the distance and have them explode.*

• *Then go back to the first steps of this exercise and repeat; this time using nicer and more pristine copies until they are 'flowing-in' on the Body.*

● *Then continue using the steps of this exercise with better and better copies (perceived as more valuable) until you can easily handle both 'in-flowing' and 'out-flowing' your best (golden or perfect) copies.*

## I : EXTERIOR VIEWPOINT

This *process* is *run* like Step-L of Section-1.

1. *"From where could you communicate to a(n) ___?"*
2. *"From where could a(n) ___ communicate to you?"*
3. *"From where could another communicate to a(n) ___?"*
4. *"From where could a(n) ___ communicate to another?"*
5. *"From where could a(n) ___ communicate to itself?"*

## J : MEMORY STORAGE

An *Alpha-Spirit* often uses *astral/spiritual*

representations of an *object-item* to store memory. In this case, the individual may use the *basic goal object-item* to store the memory of many lifetimes. This allows the *Alpha-Spirit* to "forget" ("Not-Know") them on a "conscious" level without losing them completely. Here, we *process* such *considerations*.

1. *"What memories could a(n) ___ store for you?"*

2. *"What memories could a(n) ___ store for another?"*

3. *"What memories could a(n) ___ store for others?"*

4. *"What might you allow a(n) ___ to forget?"*

**K** : THINKINGNESS

An *Alpha-Spirit* has a tendency to allow certain *object-items* (and *machinery*) to do their *thinking* for them.

1. *"What thoughts might ___ have on your behalf?"*

2. *"What thoughts could you have in the absence of ___?"*

## L : COMPULSIVE CREATION

*Run* these alternating-PCL until the *second*-PCL genuinely seems ridiculous and a *Seeker* senses that something about the *fragmentation* has "fallen away," "come apart," or some other sensation of greater "relief." Then *run* the *first*-PCL by itself several more times to stabilize the *end-point*.

1. *"From where could you create a(n) ___?"*
2. *"From where could a ___ create you?"*

## M : OBJECTIVE EXERCISE (END)

For this final exercise you will need a physical representation of the *object-item* (such as from Step-F) to hold. This is a repetitive *process*/exercise. When first *running* it, you may *perceive* the *"physical object"* in your hands as becoming *"more real"* or *"more solid"* than the rest of the room. Continue the exercise until this effect stops and/or you find yourself completely *"exterior to"* the entire entangled *energetic-mass* of the *"object-item"* (and any *fragmented significance* it represents).

This exercise is practiced with *eyes closed*, while *holding the physical object* in your hands. The actual *"spiritual perception"* (or "ZU-Vision") does not have to seem very vivid or real; just keep intending to *"mentally spot"* with your *attention*.

1. *"Spot three points in the object."*

2. *"Spot three points in the room."*

If a *Seeker* suddenly gets even a slight sense of an additional representative *copy* of the *"object-item"* off in some "strange space" or "dimension" somewhere, then add the following PCL to the series—cycling through all *three* PCL within the same *process*. Again, the vividness of perception or reality on this other *copy* does not have to be great in order to *"spot"* with *attention*.

3. *"Spot three points in the distant copy."*

---

## ADDITIONAL NOTES ON "ZU-VISION"

ZU-VISION is an imperfect term that is used in *Systemology* and *Mardukite Zuism.* Originally, the term was used to denote the experience of *Awareness* that is independent of a *Body*—and not *just* a *"Human Body"* (for the experience of *this Physical Universe*) but *any* conception of a *Body* that is restricted to *any Universe.* In the fullest sense, it is referring to the *pure unfiltered Awareness* of an *Alpha-Spirit.*

As an *exercise* or *technique,* we tend to be a little more realistic about the clarity of a *Seeker's "spiritual perception"* when ZU-Vision is handled in previous *processing-levels.* Based on what is stated in *AT Manual #1,* the form and solidity of *this Physical Universe* is being *perceived* by an

*Alpha-Spirit* through *seven-plus-one "layers"* of *Universe* reality-agreements. That certainly provides a lot of "room" for an *Alpha-Spirit* to have *compulsively fixed attention*—or *"parked"* its *Awareness*—along the way to reach *here*.

An increase of *"spiritual perception"* is a natural occurrence as a *Seeker* clears away the "debris" from these various *"layers."* Various *metaphysical* and *mystical* *"New Age"* practices tend to put a lot of emphasis and *attention* on the *"Astral Body."* This is essentially only one-*level* or one-*layer* *"up"* from *the Physical Body* (or *"genetic vehicle"*) used to conveniently experience and interact with *this Physical Universe.* The *"Astral Body"* served the same function for us in the previous (or *higher*) *"Magic Universe."*

The *"Astral Body"* is *still* a *"Body"* with *perceptions* far removed from our basic native state. That it is really only *one-degree higher* in "apparent frequency" has simply made it more accessible to individuals that have been able to access some level of higher perception using other methods.

But *"astral travel," "dream-walking"* and even *"between-lives"* periods, where we temporarily assume the *viewpoint* from our *"astral"* perspective, are not truly *"exterior to"* this *Physical Universe*—nor do they truly represent *our* practice of ZU-Vision.

Although we may access the *perception* of an *astral form*, or even enter these *viewpoints* more completely between "physical" incarnations, there are *"spiritual screens"* in place that will continue to entrap a heavily *fragmented* individual's *Awareness* to *this Universe*.

These *"screens"* are a component of the *"thought planes"* that, while quite "invisible" to normative perception, are very much present and exist *within* the confines of *this Physical Universe*. Simply *accessing* the *"Astral Body"* and operating within the *"thought planes"* is not the same as experiencing the actual *Magic Universe* with one; it just means we have *"carried"* an *Astral Body* with us down *here* as one more *layer* on top of everything else prior to it.

*Systematic Processing* (as a method of *defragmentation*) is only effective when we are treating the *Alpha-Spirit*, the actual individual themselves, and the *postulates* or *Alpha-Thought* they have established, duplicated or *agreed with*, as part of their own *Personal Universe*—or what one generally considers their *"Home Universe."*

Technically, an *Alpha-Spirit* has never actually *"left"* its original native position in a *"Home Universe."* But, it started its *creative experience* as a particularly naïve immortal *Beingness* with unlimited power. *Systematic Processing* could be applied infinitely with only marginal gains if a

*Seeker* is not being *processed* from the *viewpoint* that they are still *creating* what is experienced as their *own Universe.*

The fact that most of these *creations* are *fragmented* by innumerable layers of forgotten *reality-agreements*, or are being *automatically* and/or *reactively* "manifested" by *spiritual machinery* that has long since been "abandoned" but left active, does not change the fact that the *actual existence* of the "immortal" Alpha-Spirit remains in its *own Universe.* They are simply *assimilating* and *duplicating* the *reality* they experience based on"*impressions*" received from all of their other interactions with "*external stimuli.*"

By "*own Universe*" we literally mean "*Own,*" as in *ownership.* And with that true *ownership* comes the *total responsibility* for its *existence.* Of course, as we went along, this *responsibility* became gradually "delegated" to "outside sources"—but of which are really *fragments* of ourselves, *knowingly* set up to *do* something, and then *hidden* away from our *Knowingness*. This is why we refer quite literally to *"fragmentation* of *Awareness."*

Total *Alpha-Defragmentation* requires the *"separation"* of *"collapsed"* Universes. A *Seeker's* fundamental problem is: *agreeing* that *Beta-Existence IS Home-Universe*; and then *identifying with and as anything* in that *Beta-Existence*. When a *Seeker* solves this, they are *free* for *Ascension*.

There are varying degrees of *spiritual perception*. When first practicing with ZU-Vision—being an *Awareness*, or maintaining a *viewpoint*, just "outside" the *Body* (but still present in *Beta-Existence*)—a *Seeker* is likely *not* going to fully *perceive* the "walls" of the room. They might be able to *"imagine"* (*create mental imagery of*) them from *"memory"*; but that is not quite the same experience as having actual *spiritual perception*. This type of *invalidation* is sometimes enough to dissuade beginners from continuing a developmental practice.

There is an observed pattern that tends to occur as a *Seeker* develops *spiritual perception*. For example: first they won't be able to see the *walls*; then they can see the *walls*; and finally, they can't see the *walls* unless they first *postulate* or *agree* that there is one there.

We use *"walls"* quite often in our *objective/Universe* exercises, and for good reason: they are *agreed-upon reality barriers* that become *compulsively (unknowingly) created*. The "thing" that is *perceived* to "exist" before you is really an "order" or product of *Alpha-Thought*. It is being "ordered" to *exist*; "ordered" to *obey* a *reality-agreement* that it is *"there."*

An interesting *process* could be *run* on this point, by alternating the following PCL. [Note that its wording permits the *use of force*, but then allows one to move beyond such *considerations*.]

1. *"What wouldn't you mind obeying?"*
2. *"What would obey you?"*

\* \* \* \* \* \* \*

*High-level Awareness* is required to *confront, conceive,* or even *get the concept of,* the *actuality* of the *Alpha-Spirit.* The same can be said of *accepting* that *"Games"* are the *answer* to the ultimate *"Why?"* Such *levels* of *realization* are "beyond" the *standard-issue Human Condition.*

The fact of the matter is that *Alpha-Spirits* are fond of *games*—and they tend to prefer *"game conditions"* to *"non-game conditions."* But, *"game conditions"* require *"barriers"*; there must be some *restrictions.* The idea of *"no barriers"* or a *"total freedom of space"* are *"non-game conditions."*

*"Truth"* and *"native states"* are *non-game conditions. Fragmentation* can only result

from *game-conditions*. The *Alpha-Spirit* requires a particular level of certainty that there *"will be games."* There must be *enough barriers* to suit them. *Alpha-Spirits* become "unhappy" when *confronting* either "too many" or "too few" *barriers* for their preferred *"tolerance"* or *"involvement"* level.

Where ZU-Vision is concerned, an individual needs certainty that there will still be enough "game" in that state. The most direct method of treating this with *conceptual processing* is with alternating-PCL:

1. *"Get a sense that you can control that Body from outside it."*

2. *"Get a sense that you cannot control that Body from outside it."*

In this example of *processing* (above): one of these statements is obviously a "truth"; whereas the other is *fragmented consideration*. In actual practice, however, *running* one *or* the other by itself doesn't produce any real gains. One of the reasons for this is because there is actually a continuous "*charge*" on both *postulates* (that you both *can* and *can't*). This leads to a *suspension of Knowingness* as a "maybe" and a further reduction in *Actualized Awareness.*

*Systematic Processing* is applied to determine exactly where an individual's *attention/Awareness* has been *fixated* or *suspended* on the *Backtrack,* and then *free it.* But to do this successfully requires actually being able to *spot* what an individual is attempting to *get free from.* The *Alpha-Spirit* already *was* "*free.*" It must first consider that there is *something there* to be *free of something.* It has to *spot* "getting in" before it can "get out."

While there is plenty of *physical-matter* and *objects* in *this Physical Universe* in which to "orient" a *Physical Body,* as a *Spiritual Being,* an individual entrapped in the *Human Condition* is actually quite "lost" without properly *Backtracking* the routes by which they descended to this state.

If one truly is *seeking Ascension*, they have likely accumulated additional uncertainty by entertaining a lot of the popular routes of *"enlightenment"* that have come and gone in history, or are still with us. And perhaps the most disturbing insistence that is inherent in these "false paths" is the conception of a *"oneness"* and *"connectedness"* with the ALL-ness of *this Physical Universe*. This is an outright *lie* wrapped up in a lot of politically correct "feel good" *mysticism* that actually doesn't lead an individual anywhere but further *"in."*

If you truly want to get *"exterior to"* and *"out of"* this Physical Universe, then *process-out* any *agreement* that you are an interconnected part of it. You are simply *"remote controlling"* a *vehicle*. You are not the *vehicle*, and you are certainly not the *environment* that the *vehicle* is interacting with.

We don't *process "freedom"* (which is the *truth*), we *process "separateness"* (which is the *game-equivalent* of *freedom*). *Separateness* implies that there is *something there* to be *separate from*. Therefore, *process "barriers"* and *"separateness."*

While the subject of *"barriers"* is treated in previous *processing-levels*, the application of *"separateness"* to *processing* is not. This is quite simple as an *objective exercise*. Although we often use alternating-PCL for maintaining better control of *attention*, treating both *in-flow* and *out-flow*, and/or taking *"charge"* off of two *opposing considerations*, in this case we do *not* alternate *"separateness"* with *"connectedness."*

1. *"Spot things that are separate from you."*
2. *"Spot things you are separate from."*

At first, a *Seeker* might practice this with *eyes open* and *looking* around the room. Eventually they should shift to treating as many *objects*, *people*, and *places* that can be "spotted" (*mentally with attention*)—and with each, getting and maintaining a *sense* or *concept* of "*separateness*." *Run* this to a satisfactory *end-point*.

Your next Advanced Training manual is:
*"The Jewel of Knowledge"*

# BASIC SYSTEMOLOGY GLOSSARY

**actualization** : to make actual, not just potential; to bring into full solid Reality; to realize fully in *Awareness* as a "thing."

**agreement (reality)** : unanimity of opinion of what is "thought" to be known; an accepted arrangement of how things are; things we consider as "real" or as an "is" of "reality"; a consensus of what is real as made by standard-issue (common) participants; what an individual contributes to or accepts as "real"; in *Systemology*, a synonym for "*reality.*"

**alpha** : the first, primary, basic, superior or beginning of some form; in *Systemology*, referring to the state of existence operating on spiritual archetypes and postulates, will and intention "exterior" to the low-level condensation and solidarity of energy and matter as the 'physical universe' (*beta*).

**alpha-spirit** : a "spiritual" *Life*-form; the "true" *Self* or I-AM; the *individual*; the spiritual (*alpha*) *Self* that is animating the (*beta*) physical body or "*genetic vehicle*" using a continuous *Lifeline* of spiritual ("*ZU*") energy; an individual spiritual (*alpha*) entity possessing no physical mass or measurable waveform (motion) in the Physical Universe as itself, so it animates the (*beta*) physical body or "*genetic vehicle*" as a catalyst to experience *Self*-determined causality in effect within the *Physical Universe*; a singular unit or point of *Spiritual Awareness* that is *Aware* that it is *Aware*.

**alpha thought** : the highest spiritual *Self-determination* over creation and existence exercised by an Alpha-Spirit; the Alpha range of pure *Creative Ability* based on direct postulates and considerations of *Beingness*; spiritual qualities comparable to "thought" but originating in Alpha-existence, independently superior to a Mind-System.

**ascension** : actualized *Awareness* elevated to the point of true "spiritual existence" exterior to *beta existence*. An "Ascended Master" is one who has returned to an incarnation on Earth as an inherently *Enlightened One*, demonstrable in their words and actions; they have the ability to *Self-direct* the "Mind" and "Body" as *Self* (as a "Spirit"); and to maintain consciousness as a personal identity continuum with the same *Self-directed* control and communication of Will-Intention that is exercised, actualized and developed deliberately during one's present incarnation.

**associative knowledge** : significance or meaning of a facet or aspect assigned to (or considered to have) a direct relationship with another facet; to connect or relate ideas or facets of existence with one another; in traditional systems logic, an equivalency of significance or meaning between facets or sets that are grouped together, such as in $(a + b) + c = a + (b + c)$; in Systemology, erroneous associative knowledge is assignment of the same value to all facets or parts considered as related (even when they are not actually so), such as in $a = a,\ b = a,\ c = a$ and so forth without distinction.

**attention** : active use of *Awareness* toward a specific aspect or thing; the act of "attending" with the presence of *Self*; a direction of focus or concentration of *Awareness* along a particular channel or conduit or toward a particular terminal node or communication termination point; the Self-directed concentration of personal energy as a combination of observation, thought-waves and consideration; focused application of *Self-Directed Awareness*.

**awareness** : the highest sense of-and-as *Self* in knowing and being as I-AM (the *Alpha-Spirit*); the extent of beingness directed as a viewpoint (POV) experienced by *Self* as *Knowingness*.

**beta (awareness)** : all consciousness activity ("*Awareness*") in the "Physical Universe" (KI, in *Zuism*) or else in *beta-existence*; *Awareness* within the range of the *genetic-body*, including material thoughts, emotional responses and physical motors; personal *Awareness* of physical energy and physical matter moving through physical space and experienced as "time"; the *Awareness* held by *Self* that is restricted to an organic *Lifeform* or "*genetic vehicle*" in which it experiences causality in *beta-existence*.

**beta (existence)** : all manifestation in the "Physical Universe" (KI, in *Zuism*); the conditions of *Awareness* for the *Alpha-spirit* (*Self*) as a physical organic *Lifeform* or "*genetic vehicle*" in which it experiences causality in the *Physical Universe*.

**charge** : to fill or furnish with a quality; to supply with energy; to lay a command upon; in *Systemology*—to imbue with intention; to overspread with emotion; personal energy stores and significances entwined as fragmentation in mental images, reactive-response encoding and intellectual (and/or) programmed beliefs.

**channel** : a specific stream, course, current, direction or route; to form or cut a groove or ridge or otherwise guide along a specific course; a direct path; an artificial aqueduct created to connect two water bodies or water or make travel possible.

**circuit** : a circular path or loop; a closed-path within a system that allows a flow; a pattern or action or wave movement that follows a specific route or potential path only; in *Systemology*, "*communication processing*" pertaining to a specific *flow* of energy or information along a channel; "*feedback loop.*"

**communication** : successful transmission of information, data, energy (&tc.) along a message line, with a reception of feedback; an energetic flow of intention to cause an effect (or duplication) at a distance; the personal energy moved or acted upon by will or else 'selective directed attention'; the 'messenger action' used to transmit and receive energy across a medium; also relay of energy, a message or signal—or even locating a personal POV (viewpoint) for the Self—along the *ZU-line.*

**condense (condensation)** : the transition of vapor to liquid; denoting a change in state to a more substantial or solid condition; leading to a more compact or solid form.

**confront** : to come around in front of; to be in the presence of; to stand in front of, or in the face of; to meet "face-to-face" or "face-up-to"; additionally, in *Systemology*, to fully tolerate or acceptably withstand an encounter with a particular manifestation without an automatic reactive response.

**consideration** : careful analytical reflection of all aspects; deliberation; determining the significance of a "thing" in relation to similarity or dissimilarity to other "things"; evaluation of facts and importance of certain facts; thorough examination of all aspects related to, or important for, making a decision; the analysis of consequences and estimation of significance when making decisions; also in *Systemology*, the *postulate* or *Alpha-Thought* that defines the state of *beingness* for what something "*is.*"

**defragmentation** : the *reparation* of wholeness; collecting all dispersed parts to reform an original whole; a process of removing "*fragmentation*" in data or knowledge to provide a clear understanding; applying techniques and processes that promote a *holistic* interconnected *alpha* state, favoring observational *Awareness* of continuity in all spiritual and physical systems; in *Systemology*, a "*Seeker*" achieving actualized "*Self-Honest Awareness*" is said to be in a basic state of *beta-defragmentation*, whereas *Alpha-defragmentation* is the rehabilitation of the *creative ability*, managing the *Spiritual Timeline* and the POV of *Self* as Alpha-Spirit (I-AM).

**existence** : the *state* or fact of *apparent manifestation*; the resulting combination of the Principles of Manifestation: consciousness, motion and substance; continued *survival*; that which independently exists.

**exterior** : outside of; on the outside; in *Systemology*, we mean specifically the POV of *Self* that is *'outside of'* the *Human Condition*, free of the physical and mental trappings of the Physical Universe; a metahuman range of consideration; see also *'Zu-Vision'*.

**external** : a force coming from outside; information received from outside sources; in *Systemology*, the objective *'Physical Universe'* existence, or *beta-existence*, that the Physical Body or *genetic vehicle* is essentially *anchored* to for its considerations of locational space-time as a dimension or POV.

**fragmentation** : breaking into parts and scattering the pieces; the *fractioning* of wholeness or the *fracture* of a holistic interconnected *alpha* state, favoring observational *Awareness* of perceived connectivity between parts; *discontinuity*; separation of a totality into parts; in *Systemology*, a person outside of *Self-Honesty* is said to be operating from a *fragmented* state.

**flow** : movement across (or through) a channel (or conduit); a direction of active energetic motion, typically distinguished as either an *in-flow*, *out-flow* or *cross-flow*.

**genetic-vehicle** : a physical *Life*-form; the physical (*beta*) body that is animated/controlled by the (*Alpha*) *Spirit* using a continuous *Spiritual Lifeline* (ZU); a physical (*beta*) organic receptacle and catalyst for the (*Alpha*) *Self* to operate "causes" and experience "effects" within the *Physical Universe*.

**harmful-act** : a counter-survival mode of behavior or action (esp. that causes harm to one of more *Spheres of Existence*)—or—an overtly aggressive (hostile and/or destructive) action against an individual or any other *Sphere of Existence*; in *Utilitarian Systemology*—a short-sighted (serves fewest/lowest *Spheres of Existence*) intentional overtly harmful action to resolve a perceived problem; a revision of the rule for standard *Utilitarianism* for Systemology to distinguish actions which provide the least benefit to the least number of *Spheres of Existence*, or else the greatest harm to the greatest number of *Spheres of Existence*; in *moral philosophy*—an action which can be experienced by few and/or which one would not be willing to experience for themselves (*theft, slander, rape, &tc*); an iniquity or iniquitous act.

**hold-back** : withheld communications (esp. actions) such as "*Hold-Outs*"; intentional (or automatic) withdrawal (as opposed to reach); Self-restraint (which may eventually be enforced or automated); not reaching, acting or expressing, when one should be; an ability that is now restrained (on automatic) due to inability to withhold it on Self-determinism alone.

**hold-outs** : in photography, the numerous snap-shots/pictures withheld from the final display or professional presentation of the event; withheld communications; in Utilitarian Systemology—energetic withdrawal and communication breaks with a "*terminal*" and its *Sphere of Existence* as a result of a "*Harmful-Act*"; unspoken or undiscovered (hidden, covert) actions that an individual withholds communications of, fearing punishment or endangerment of *Self-preservation* (*First Sphere*); the act of hiding (or keeping hidden) the truth of a "*Harmful-Act*"; a refusal to communicate with a *Pilot*; also "*Hold-Back.*"

**holistic** : the examination of interconnected systems as encompassing something greater than the *sum* of their "parts."

**Human Condition** : a standard default state of Human experience that is generally accepted to be the extent of its potential identity (*beingness*) —currently treated as *Homo Sapiens Sapiens,* but which is scheduled for replacement by *Homo Novus* (the "New Human").

**imagination** : ability to create *mental imagery* in one's Personal Universe at will and change or alter it as desired; the ability to create, change and dissolve mental images on command or as an act of will; to create a mental image or have associated imagery displayed (or "conjured") in the mind that may or may not be treated as real (or memory recall) and may or may not accurately duplicate objective reality; to employ *creative abilities* of the Spirit that are independent of reality agreements with beta-existence.

**imprint** : to strongly impress, stamp, mark (or outline) onto a softer 'impressible' substance; to mark with pressure onto a surface; in *Systemology*, used to indicate permanent Reality impressions marked by frequencies, energies or interactions experienced during periods of emotional distress, pain, unconsciousness, loss, enforcement, or something antagonistic to physical (personal) survival, all of which are are stored with other reactive response-mechanisms at lower-levels of *Awareness* as opposed to the active memory database and proactive processing center of the Mind; an experiential "memory-set" that may later resurface—be triggered or stimulated artificially—as Reality, of which similar responses will be engaged automatically; holographic-like imagery "stamped" onto consciousness as composed of energetic *facets* tied to the "snap-shot" of an experience.

**imprinting incident** : the first or original event

instance communicated and *emotionally en-coded* onto an individual's "*Spiritual Timeline*" (recorded memory from all lifetimes), which formed a permanent impression that is later used to mechanistically treat future contact on that channel; the first or original occurrence of some particular *facet* or mental image related to a certain type of *encoded response*, such as pain and discomfort, losses and victimization, and even the acts that we have taken against others along the *Spiritual Timeline* of our existence that caused them to also be *Imprinted*.

**intention** : directed application of Will; to intend (have "in Mind") or signify (give "significance" to) for or toward a particular purpose; in *Systemology* (from the *Standard Model*)—the spiritual activity at WILL (5.0) directed by an *Alpha Spirit* (7.0); the application of WILL as "Cause" from a higher order of Alpha Thought and consideration (6.0).

**interior** : inside of; on the inside; in *Systemology*, we mean specifically the POV of *Self* that is fixed to the *'internal' Human Condition,* including the *Reactive Control Center* (RCC) and Mind-System or *Master Control Center* (MCC); within *beta-existence*.

**internal** : a force coming from inside; information received from inside sources; in *Systemology*, the objective experience of *beta-existence* associated with the Physical Body or *genetic vehicle* and its POV regarding sensation and perception; from inside the body; in the body.

**invalidate** : decrease the level or degree or *agreement* as Reality.

**mental image** : a subjectively experienced "picture" created and imagined into being by the Alpha-Spirit (or at lower levels, one of its automated mechanisms) that includes all perceptible *facets* of totally immersive scene, which may be forms originated by an individual, or a "facsimile-copy" ("snap-shot") of something seen or encountered; a duplication of wave-forms in one's Personal Universe as a "picture" that mirror an "external" Universe experience, such as an *Imprint*.

**perception** : internalized processing of data received by the *senses*; to become *Aware of* via the senses.

**pilot** : a professional steersman responsible for healthy functional operation of a ship toward a specific destination; in *Systemology*, an intensive trained individual qualified to specially apply *Systemology Processing* to assist other *Seekers* on the *Pathway*.

**point-of-view (POV)** : a point to view from; an opinion or attitude as expressed from a specific identity-phase; a specific standpoint or vantage-point; a definitive manner of consideration specific to an individual phase or identity; a place or position affording a specific view or vantage; circumstances and programming of an individual that is conducive to a particular response, consideration or belief-set (paradigm); a position (consideration) or place (location) that provides a specific view or perspective (subjective) on experience (of the objective).

**postulate** : to put forward as truth; to suggest or assume an existence *to be*; to state or affirm the existence of particular conditions; to provide a basis of reasoning and belief; a basic theory accepted as fact; in *Systemology*, Alpha-Thought —the top-most decisions or considerations made by the Alpha-Spirit regarding the "*is-ness*" (what things "are") about energy-matter and space-time.

**presence** : a quality of some thing (*energy/matter*) being "present" in space-time; personal orientation of *Self* as an *Awareness* (*POV*) located in present space-time (environment) and communicating with extant energy-matter.

**processing command line (PCL)** : a directed input; a specific command using highly selective language for *Systemology Processing*; a predetermined directive statement (cause) intended to focus concentrated attention (effect).

**processing, systematic** : the inner-workings or "through-put" result of systems; in *Systemology*, a method of applied spiritual technology used toward personal Self-Actualization; methods of selective directed attention, communicated language and associative imagery that increases personal control of the human condition.

**realization** : the clear perception of an understanding; a consideration or understanding on what is "actual"; to make "real" or give "reality" to so as to grant a property of "beingness" or "being as it is"; the state or instance of coming to an *Awareness*; in *Systemology*, "gnosis" or true knowledge achieved during *systematic processing*; achievement of a new (or higher) cognition, true knowledge or perception of Self; a consideration of reality or assignment of meaning.

**responsibility** : the *ability* to *respond*; the extent of mobilizing *power* and *understanding* an individual maintains as *Awareness* to enact *change*; the proactive ability to *Self-direct* and make decisions independent of an outside authority.

**Seeker** : an individual on the *Pathway to Self-Honesty*; a practitioner of *Mardukite Systemology* or *Systemology Processing*, that is working toward *Spiritual Ascension*.

**Self-actualization** : bringing the full potential of the Human spirit into Reality; expressing full capabilities and creativeness of the *Alpha-Spirit*.

**Self-determinism** : the freedom to act, clear of external control or influence; the personal control of Will to direct intention.

**Self-honesty** : the basic or original *alpha* state of *being* and *knowing*; clear and present total *Awareness* of-and-as *Self*, in its most basic and true proactive expression of itself as *Spirit* or *I-AM*—free of artificial attachments, perceptive filters and other emotionally-reactive or mentally-conditioned programming imposed on the human condition by the systematized physical world; the ability to experience existence without judgment.

**spiritual timeline** : a continuous stream of moment-to-moment *Mental Images* (or a record of experiences) that defines the "past" of a spiritual being (or *Alpha-Spirit*) and which includes impressions (*imprints, &tc.*) from all life-incarnations and significant spiritual events the being has encountered; in Systemology, also "*backtrack.*"

**Spheres of Existence** : a series of *eight* concentric circles, rings or spheres (each larger than the former) that is overlaid onto the Standard Model of Beta-Existence to demonstrate the dynamic systems of existence extending out from the POV of Self (often as a "body") at the *First Sphere*; these are given in the basic eightfold systems as: *Self, Home/Family, Groups, Humanity, Life on Earth, Physical Universe, Spiritual Universe* and *Infinity-Divinity.*

**Systemology** : a modern tradition of applied religious philosophy and spiritual technology based on *Arcane Tablets* (in combination with "*general systemology*" and "*games theory*") developed in the New Age underground by Joshua Free in 2011 as an advanced futurist extension of the *Mardukite Research Org.*

**terminal (node)** : a point, end, or mass, on a line; a connection point for closing an electric circuit, such as a post on a battery terminating at each end of its own systematic function; a point of connectivity with other points; in systems, a contact point of interaction; a point of interaction with other points.

**turbulence** : a quality or state of distortion or disturbance that creates irregularity of a flow or pattern; the quality or state of aberration on a line (such as ragged edges) or the emotional "turbulent feelings" attached to a particular flow or terminal node; a violent, haphazard or disharmonious commotion (such as in the ebb of gusts and lulls of wind action).

**validation** : a reinforcement of agreements or considerations as being "real."

**viewpoint** : see *"point-of-view" (POV)*.

**willingness** : the state of conscious Self-determined ability and interest (directed attention) to *Be*, *Do* or *Have*; a Self-determined consideration to reach, face up to (*confront*) or manage some "mass" or energy; the extent to which an individual considers themselves able to participate, act or communicate along some line, to put attention or intention on the line, or to produce (create) an effect.

**ZU** : the ancient Sumerian cuneiform sign for the archaic verb—*"to know,"* *"knowingness"* or *"awareness"*; in *Mardukite Zuism and Systemology*, the active energy/matter of the "Spiritual Universe" (AN) experienced as a *Lifeforce* or *consciousness* that imbues living forms extant in the "Physical Universe" (KI); *"Spiritual Life Energy"*; energy demonstrated by the WILL of an actualized *Alpha-Spirit* in the "Spiritual Universe" (AN), which impinges its *Awareness* into the Physical Universe (KI), animating/controlling *Life* for its experience of *beta-existence* along an individual Alpha-Spirit's personal *Identity-continuum*, called a *ZU-line*.

**Zu-Line** : a theoretical construct in *Mardukite Zuism and Systemology* demonstrating *Spiritual*

*Life Energy* (*ZU*) as a personal individual "continuum" of Awareness interacting with all Spheres of Existence on the Standard Model of Systemology; a spectrum of potential variations and interactions of a monistic continuum or singular *Spiritual Life Energy* demonstrated on the Standard Model; an energetic channel of potential POV and "locations" of Beingness, demonstrated in early Systemology materials as an individual Alpha-Spirit's personal *Identity- continuum*, potentially connecting *Awareness* of *Self* with "*Infinity*" simultaneous with all points considered in existence; a symbolic demonstration of the "*Life-line*" on which *Awareness (ZU)* extends from the direction of the "Spiritual Universe" (AN) in its true original *alpha state* through an entire possible range of activity resulting in its *beta state* and control of a *genetic-entity* occupying the *Physical Universe (KI).*

**Zu-Vision** : the true and basic (*Alpha*) Point-of-View (perspective, POV) maintained by *Self* as *Alpha-Spirit* outside boundaries or considerations of the *Human Condition* and *exterior* to beta-existence reality agreements with the Physical Universe; a POV of Self *as* "a unit of Spiritual Awareness" that exists independent of a "body" and entrapment in a *Human Condition*; "spirit vision" in its truest sense.

*Collector's Edition Hardcover*

# THE FUNDAMENTALS OF
# SYSTEMOLOGY

A Basic Course developed by
Joshua Free

*collecting material of six lesson-booklets
together in one volume!*

*"Being More Than Human"*

*"Realities in Agreement"*

*"Windows To Experience"*

*"Ancient Systemology"*

*"A History of Systemology"*

*"Systemology Processing"*

All *six* lesson-booklets of the first official
*Basic Course* on Mardukite Systemology
are combined together in *one volume* as
*"Fundamentals of Systemology."*

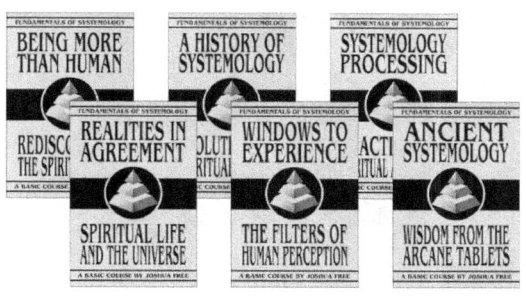

*Lesson booklets are also available individually!*

*Collector's Edition Hardcover*

# THE PATHWAY TO
# ASCENSION

The Systemology
Professional Course by
Joshua Free

*All sixteen lessons available in two volumes!*

*"Increasing Awareness"*

*"Thought & Emotion"*

*"Clear Communication"*

*"Handling Humanity"*

*"Free Your Spirit"*

*"Escaping Spirit-Traps"*

*"Eliminating Barriers"*

*"Conquest of Illusion"*

...and more!

All *sixteen* lesson-booklets of the newest
*Professional Course* on Mardukite Systemology
are combined together in *two volumes* as
*"The Pathway to Ascension."*

*Lesson booklets are also available individually!*

# THE SYSTEM

Seekers and students of the *Professional Course* and *Advanced Training Course* will also be interested in the original *Systemology Core Research Series*. These *8* volumes are a complete chronological record of *Mardukite NexGen New Thought* developments published by the *Systemology Society* from 2019 through 2023.

*The Systemology Core* series begins with the first professional publication released when our *Mardukite Systemology* emerged from the underground in 2019, with: *"The Tablets of Destiny Revelation."*

# OLOGY CORE

The Tablets of Destiny Revelation:
*How Long-Lost Anunnaki Wisdom*
*Can Change the Fate of Humanity*

Crystal Clear: *Handbook for Seekers*

Metahuman Destinations (*2 volumes*)

Imaginomicon:
*Approaching Gateways to Higher Universes*

Way of the Wizard: *Utilitarian Systemology*

Systemology-180: *Fast-Track to Ascension*

Systemology Backtrack:
*Reclaiming Spiritual Power & Past-Life Memory*

PUBLISHED BY THE **JOSHUA FREE** IMPRINT REPRESENTING

## The Mardukite Academy of Systemology

**THE JOSHUA FREE IMPRINT**
**JFI PUBLICATIONS**

**MARDUKITE**
**ZUISM**

**mardukite.com**

www.ingramcontent.com/pod-product-compliance
Lightning Source LLC
Chambersburg PA
CBHW071154120626
46546CB00006B/2262